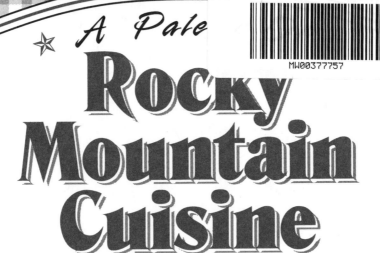

A Palate for
Rocky Mountain Cuisine

Classic Recipes
from the
Historic Hotels
of the Rocky
Mountain West

By John D. Feinberg
(Editor of Recipes / Author of Text)

AHH-West Publishing ✶ Boulder, Colorado

A Palette of Rocky Mountain Cuisine: Classic Recipes From the Historic Hotels of the Rocky Mountain West

Published by:
The Association of Historic Hotels
of the Rocky Mountain West
AHH-WEST
1002 Walnut, Suite 201
Boulder, Colorado 80302
(303) 546-9040

Editor of Recipes and Author of Text: John D. Feinberg

Cover Photograph by: John Weiland, *Photo,Graphic,Art*

Graphic Design by: Bob Schram, *Bookends*, 1245 Pearl Street, Boulder, CO 80302

Word Processing and Layout by: Juliette R. Lennon

Hotel illustrations are from original hotel archives; remaining illustrations are by Allyn Feinberg and John Feinberg.

Poetry by: Christie Burch

ISBN No.: 0-923280-01-4

Printed in the United States of America

Preface

Rocky Mountain Cuisine has been evolving for many centuries. It is an amalgam of native ingredients, and the native's and immigrant's cultural cuisines. Its early days were influenced heavily by the people of the pueblos of the Southwest, the Spanish from Mexico, and the French and English fur trappers and adventurers. It continued with Chinese railroad workers, Basque sheepherders, and waves of immigrants from Scandinavia, England, Germany, and Italy.

Rocky Mountain Cuisine flourished in supply towns at the base of the Rockies, in the adobe villages along the Rio Grande Valley and Santa Fe trail, in the gold mining camps deep in the Rockies, and the cowboy's line camps up near timberline. Rocky Mountain Cuisine reached its high point in the classic hotels. It still does.

The recipes presented here are from the last decade of the twentieth century. They represent the skills of some of the finest chefs in the West, who draw upon native and imported ingredients and marry these ingredients with the rich cultural traditions of the West. Each chef brings his or her own style to their offerings. Yet each is representative of a cuisine which is distinctive in its own right.

I wish to share with you the special recipes of my friends who hold "court" at the restaurants of the finest historic hotels in the Rocky Mountains, from the southern tip of the American Rockies at The Lodge in Cloudcroft, New Mexico, to the northern tip at the Izaak Walton Inn adjacent to Glacier National Park in Essex, Montana.

The chefs tell their story through their cuisine. Ernie at The Lodge is a regular award winner, greatly influenced by both the new southwestern and classic continental cuisine. Lynda at the Izaak has evolved a cuisine based on the best of Montana ranch cooking, with folks coming more than 150 miles to dine at her table. Each of the other featured chefs, and the hotel restaurants, enjoy favored status among those who enjoy fresh ingredients, lovingly prepared, in the style of the cuisine of the Rocky Mountains.

In order to provide a few more flavorings as you read through our cookbook, I've written about some of the interesting native ingredients, a bit of history about cuisine in the Rockies, and tried to provide a glimpse of the various people who have settled the country. True spice has been added by our good friend Christine Burch, cowgirl poet of the Historic Redstone Inn of Redstone, Colorado, who provides her personal interpretation of dining and cooking with the cowboys.

The book is organized by historic hotel from the southern portion of the Rocky Mountain Time Zone, working our way north. Each hotel's recipes are organized by course, from appetizer to dessert.

I believe this book will bring you both delight and joy in its reading and your dining.

Acknowledgments

I'd like to take this moment to thank all of my good friends who were an integral part of the effort to put this cookbook together. It's truly a group effort. First and foremost, I'd like to extend a sincere thanks to all the superb chefs at the fine historic hotels for sharing so many of their favorite signature recipes. I'm always in awe of their enormous talent. I also want to thank them for allowing me to spend time in their kitchens, learning new techniques, and additional trade secrets. I definitely appreciate being given the opportunity to be guest chef at the hotels, or at a gathering of all of us.

This cookbook was not complete without the fabulous cowgirl poetry of Christy, who tends to "roast" me with poetry at our gatherings. One day, I'll get creative enough to roast her back. I want to thank Allyn Feinberg for the delightful illustrations, and extend a lifetime of appreciation for the patience shown through the years at turning my word scrambles into edited, coherent thoughts. Juliette Lennon has put in huge numbers of hours at word processing, recipe rustling, browbeating chefs, and just plain managing. An equally huge thank you is her due. The talented Master Chef, Gary St. Clair of the Peck House, winner of the Governor's Award for excellence in serving and promotion of Colorado food products, used his abundant talents to recheck recipes for accuracy, a difficult job well done by a close friend.

We were able to cajole Duncan Hansson into dragging himself away from carpentering long enough to create the monster palette, which graces the cover, and John Weiland away from photographing the Olympic ski team long enough to come down off the hill and photograph Gary St. Clair for the cover. Many thanks to all three. It looks great. Also deep appreciation to Kak Slick for her suggestion of the name of the book, it really tells the story of the variety and artistry in the cuisine.

Bob Schram took the manuscript and made it into art. His firm, *Bookends*, created wonderful "plate presentation"! We appreciate his talent and thank him for his attention to detail. It has been marvelous to work with Johnson Publishing. They've been an institution in the Rockies for years and love to bring its culture to the attention of the world. They are true pros.

Lastly, this book would never have occurred without the support of the member hotels of the Association of Historic Hotels of the Rocky Mountain West. This collection of prestigious historic hotels is only matched by the people who own and manage these fine establishments. The quality shows in their dedication to guest service, telling the history of the Rocky Mountain West through their hotels, in their respect for their hotels, and their fine Rocky Mountain cuisine.

And, to you the reader, many thanks for giving us a try. Prepare some repasts from these recipes, come out and visit with us a spell and immerse yourself in fine hotels, fine Rocky Mountain cuisine, and the history and charm that is so distinctly the Rockies.

Southern Region

Central Region

Northern Region

A stay in The Lodge is a step back in time to a more gracious, relaxed and pleasant occasion than can be found at modern resorts. The Lodge is perched at 9,200 feet atop New Mexico's Southern Rockies in the historic mountain railroad village of Cloudcroft, and is dressed in rich wood moldings, turn-of-the-century furniture, antique fixtures, mounted game, and paddle fans. One of the Lodge's most interesting features is its copper-domed observatory, with a tower view stretching 150 miles across the shimmering dunes of the White Sands National Monument. Rocky Mountain cuisine, prepared by New Mexico's most award-winning chef, attracts guests from throughout the Southwest. There are also banquet and conference rooms ready for important occasions, whether personal or corporate. The unique natural setting and wilderness spirit of The Lodge is best reflected in its rustic backdrop: a mountain land of verdant pine, blue spruce, and golden aspen, wild bears, and grazing elk. The fiery sunsets and star-bright nights welcome visitors from around the world.

#1 Corona Place, Cloudcroft, NM / Phone: 1-505-682-2566, 1-800-395-6343, Fax: 1-505-682-2715

Cloudcroft ⋆ NEW MEXICO ⋆ 47 Rooms

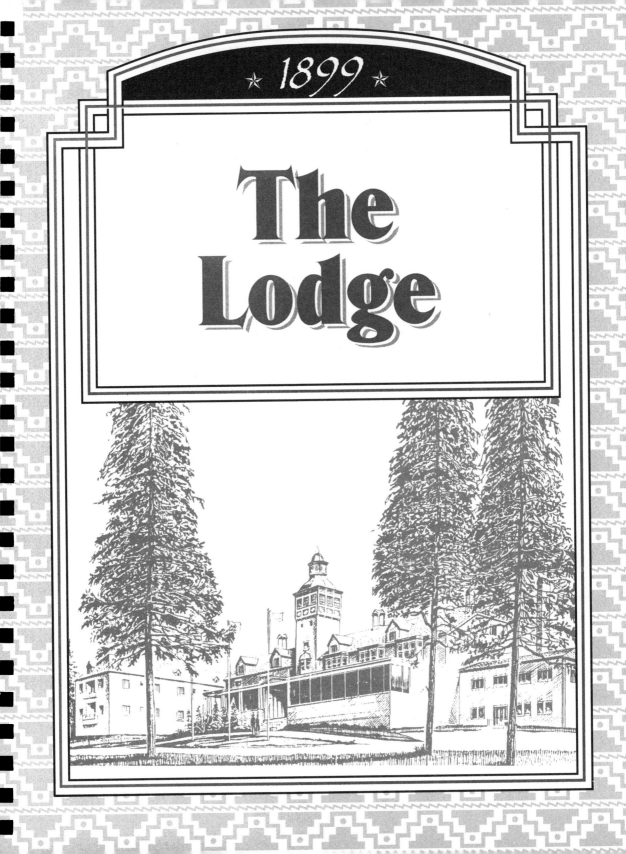

1899

The Lodge

Mushroom Caps with Mussels in Brandy Cream Sauce

8	Mushroom caps, large, cleaned, stems removed
8	Mussels, fresh, cleaned, steamed, removed from shell
1 T.	Butter
1 T.	Garlic, finely minced
1 T.	Shallots, finely minced
1/4 c.	Mussel broth
1/4 c.	Heavy cream
2 oz.	Brandy
1 T.	Chives, chopped
1	Red bell pepper, diced

Sauté mushroom caps in whole butter and remove from pan. Add garlic and shallots to pan, sauté until lightly browned. Add mussel broth, heavy cream, brandy, and chopped chives.

Reduce to thicken. Add mushrooms, mussels, and warm. On plate, fill each mushroom cap with a mussel, top with sauce and garnish with diced red bell pepper or garnish of your choice.

Makes Two Servings

Orange Slaw with Sweet Water

1	Napa cabbage, head , shredded
1	Raddicchio, head, shredded
1	Mandarin Orange segments, small can, drained

DRESSING:

1/2 c.	Water
1/4 c.	Shin Mirin (found in Oriental specialty stores)
1/4 c.	Sake
1/4 c.	Rice wine vinegar
2 T.	Sugar

Mix cabbage, raddicchio, oranges. Toss lightly with dressing until coated.

In a small saucepan, heat but do not boil the water, Shin Mirin, Sake, wine vinegar and sugar, until sugar is dissolved, then cool.

Makes Eight Servings

"This soup is my invention. It's something I make when I need to use up leftover chicken stock. I have made this soup many times, and it always comes out different because I put leftover items in it. But, I think that this recipe is very close to the basic one."

"The flavor is fairly hot, but not too spicy. The jalapeños give it a nice bite. Be sure to remove the seeds. Otherwise, you will burn your lips, unless you are used to the hotness." (Ernie Bolleter, executive Chef at The Lodge.)

You can have this as a whole meal, it's so filling. Just serve it with a good bread or some corn tortillas.

In a large heavy soup pot, place the chicken, water, and salt. Bring the water to a boil and then reduce it to a simmer. Skim the foam off the top. Add the bay leaves, peppercorns, and the stems and ends of the vegetables. Cook for 1 hour, or until the chicken is done.

Remove the chicken from the pot and let it cool. Skin and bone the chicken. Cut it into small chunks. Strain the chicken broth through a sieve and pour it back in the pot.

In a large skillet, place the bacon grease and heat it on medium until it is hot. Add the flour and stir it until it is lightly browned. Add the resultant roux to the broth. Add the celery, tomatoes, scallions, jalapeños, onion, and bell peppers to the broth. Cook 30 minutes, or until the vegetables are barely done.

Add the chicken, zucchini, avocados, and corn. Cook them for 5 minutes. Correct the seasoning, if necessary.

Garnish with the blue corn tortilla chips.

Makes Eight Servings

1	Chicken, whole, 3 lb.
2 qt.	Water
1 t.	Salt
2	Bay leaves
1 t.	Peppercorns

(Save the ends and stems from the following vegetables)

6	Celery, stalks, diced
3	Tomatoes, peeled, seeded, and diced
1	Scallion, bunch, sliced
2	Jalapeño peppers, seeded and chopped
1	Onion, medium, chopped
3	Green bell peppers, seeded, washed, and diced
1/2 c.	Bacon grease
3/4 c.	Flour
2	Zucchinis, small, diced
2	Avocados, quartered and sliced
1 c.	Whole Corn
	Blue Corn Tortilla Chips

Veal and Shrimp Thermidor

"This recipe was created when I had some veal and shrimp left over. It's a hot, spicy dish, but the Marsala gives it a nice, sweet flavor. It's important to use the brand I've suggested. I've tried a lot of other kinds and this is the only one that tastes right.

You serve the sauce over the veal and shrimp, on top of the rice. It's delicious!" (Ernie Bolleter, executive chef at The Lodge)

2 T.	Butter
24 oz.	Veal fillet, sliced into 1/8" pieces
24	Shrimp, medium, peeled and deveined
1/2 t.	Salt
2 t.	Paprika
1/2 t.	Cayenne pepper
1 T.	Flour
1/2 c.	Dry Florio Marsala (no substitution)
1-1/2 c.	Heavy cream
3 c.	White rice, cooked

In a large skillet, place the butter and heat it on medium until it melts. Add the veal and sauté for 1 to 2 minutes. Add the shrimp and sauté for 1 minute.

Add the salt, paprika, and cayenne pepper. Stir everything together. Add the flour and sauté for 1 minute.

Add the Marsala and reduce the sauce by 1/3. Add the cream and simmer until the sauce has the consistency of heavy cream.

Serve over rice.

Makes Four Servings

Rebecca Freeze

Ms Nosi Crosby, a long-time staff favorite and celebrity at The Lodge, created this delicious signature after-dinner dessert cocktail.

3	French Vanilla ice cream, scoops
1-1/2 oz.	Praline Liqueur
1 oz.	White Cream de Cacao
	Piñon nuts, toasted, ground

Blend thoroughly. Serve in frozen champagne flute, top with ground toasted piñon nuts.

Makes One Serving

Breaded Sesame Seed Cod with Sweet/Spicy Bananas

"When you cook the bananas, you must be careful not to break them when you turn them over. And, do not let them get mushy or they will not look good (but they will still taste good). The sauce is really delicious because some of the bananas will get into it, and then it gets nice and creamy."

Sprinkle the cod with the salt and black pepper. Pour the lime juice over the cod fillets and let them marinate for 15 minutes at room temperature. Preheat oven to 350 degrees.

In a small bowl, place the bread crumbs and sesame seeds, and mix them together. Dip the fillets first in the flour, next in the beaten eggs, and then in the bread crumb-sesame seed mixture.

In a large skillet, place the vegetable oil and heat it on medium high until it is hot. Add the breaded fish fillets and sauté them for 2 minutes on each side, or until they are a light, golden brown. Place the breaded, sautéed cod fillets in a pan and bake them for 10 minutes, or until they are just done (turn them over once).

On each of four individual serving plates, place a cod fillet. Place one Sweet and Spicy Sautéed Banana on top. Pour on some of the sauce from the bananas.

Garnish the plate with a lime wedge.

In a medium skillet, place the butter and heat it on medium high until it has melted and is hot. Add the bananas and sauté them for 20 seconds on each side.

Add the chile caribe, honey, and lime juice. Remove the pan from the heat and swirl it around (without breaking the bananas) so that the honey, butter, and lime juice bind to form a smooth mixture.

Makes Four Servings

BREADED SESAME SEED COD:

4	Cod fillets, 6 oz.
	Salt and pepper (to taste)
1/4 c.	Lime juice, freshly squeezed
3/4 c.	Bread crumbs
1/2 c.	Sesame seeds
1/2 c.	Flour (or as needed)
2	Eggs, lightly beaten
1/2 c.	Vegetable oil
	Sweet and Spicy Sautéed Bananas (recipe below)
1	Lime, quartered

SWEET AND SPICY SAUTÉED BANANAS:

3 T.	Sweet butter
2	Bananas (ripe but firm), peeled and sliced in half both ways
2 t.	Chile Caribe (crushed red chile peppers)
2 T.	Honey
1/2	Lime, freshly squeezed

Fresh Peaches with Almond Cream

"The peaches that you use must be nice and ripe, preferably ones that are locally grown. A canned peach would be better than a bad, fresh one. This recipe will work with fresh pears, also, which are usually available all year round."

"The only reason for putting the peaches in the sugar water is to keep them fresh until you are ready to serve them. This is a very rich, delicious dessert! It tastes yummy!"

2-1/2 c.	Milk, heated
1 t.	Vanilla
4	Egg yolks
1/2 c.	Flour
1-1/4 c.	Sugar
1 c.	Sugar
2 c.	Almonds, sliced, toasted
1 pt.	Whipping cream
3/4 c.	Simple syrup (1/2 c. sugar dissolved in 1/2 c. water)
3	Peaches, ripe, blanched, peeled, halved, and pitted

In a medium saucepan, place the milk and vanilla, and heat them on medium. In a medium bowl, place the egg yolks, flour, and the 1-1/4 c. of sugar. Mix them together. Add the hot milk, while whisking rapidly to prevent lumping.

Pour the mixture back into the saucepan that contained the hot milk. Place it over a medium heat and stir constantly until the custard is thick and creamy. Set it aside to cool.

In a small saucepan place the 1 c. of sugar and heat it slowly until the sugar melts and turns a golden brown. In a shallow baking pan, place the almond slices. Pour the caramelized sugar over the almonds. Let it harden.

Break up the hardened caramel almond and place it in the center of a terry cloth towel. Bring the ends together and twist them. Beat the caramel almond with a wooden mallet, until it is finely crushed.

Add all but 1/2 c. of the crushed candy to the custard mixture and mix it in. In a medium bowl, place the whipping cream and beat it until soft peaks form. Fold half of the whipped cream into the custard mixture. In a small bowl, place the simple syrup mixture. Add the peaches and let them soak for 30 minutes.

Place some of the caramel custard mixture into the bottom of 6 champagne glasses. Place the peach halves, upside down, over the custard.

Garnish with the rest of the whipped cream and the candy.

Makes Six Servings

Peaches

Peaches are grown in the rich soil of south-facing slopes of the valleys throughout the Rockies. Sometimes the valleys are very large, such as the Valley of the Rio Grande through New Mexico, and sometimes they are small, little side-valleys, with a warmer microclimate and water for irrigation. The Navajo tribe had just such a fine valley, with canyon walls to reflect the heat and extend the growing season. This valley was the site of their peach orchard, whose peaches sustained them throughout the year, as they dried them for the winter months.

The Navajos have large flocks of sheep, which requires that they live far from each other to have land to graze, both summer and winter. As a result of being so dispersed, as opposed to being gathered together in pueblos or villages, the federal government in Washington had a very hard time figuring out how to subjugate these proud people. Finally, Kit Carson was asked to do the job.

Kit Carson is believed to have known of the peach orchards beforehand. A substantial number of the Navajo were captured, and Kit Carson cut down their beautiful orchards, then marched them from their lands. Afterward, Washington saw that a settled and peaceful people had been transplanted to a land without identity for the Navajo, in which sheep could not find grass to eat, and peaches did not have warm fertile valley floors to grow in. Washington finally realized that this was a mistake, and back the Navajo went to their land, to their four sacred mountains, to their grass, and to their valley to grow peaches.

The Old Town Plaza in Las Vegas, New Mexico, was once the most important mercantile stop on the Santa Fe Trail. Las Vegas became a regular stop for ranchers, miners, bankers, bunko artists, card sharks, gamblers, "lost" women, and desperados. Infamous characters of the Wild West like Billy the Kid, Doc Holliday and Black Jack Ketchum became frequent visitors and helped earn Las Vegas a reputation as one of the rowdiest cities in the West. The Plaza Hotel was built following the arrival of the Atchinson, Topeka and Santa Fe Railroad. Constructed in the Italianate-bracketed style, it was soon described as the "Belle of the Southwest." The Plaza offers both Victorian charm and contemporary comfort, with spacious guest rooms, fine dining, and a lively saloon awaiting the adventurous traveler. Exceptional side trips include Fort Union and Pecos National Monuments, The Rough Riders Museum, Gallinas Canyon, and Armand Hammer United World College. Las Vegas offers many summer and winter sport activities.

230 Old Town Plaza, Las Vegas, NM / Phone: 1-505-425-3591, 1-800-328-1882, Fax: 1-505-425-9659

Las Vegas ★ NEW MEXICO ★ 38 Rooms

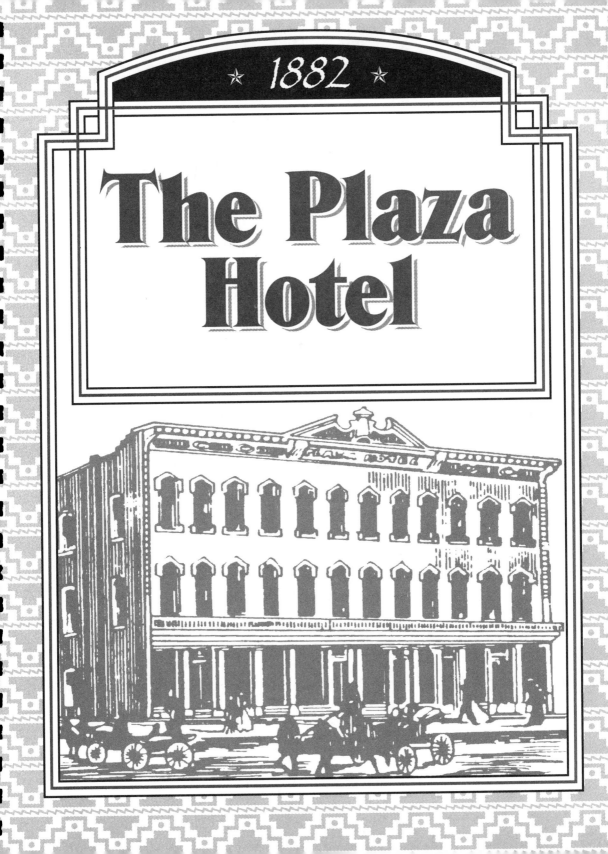

The Plaza Hotel

1882

Chilled Shrimp with Raspberry Salsa

1 lb. Shrimp, medium, shelled, deveined, cooked and chilled

RASPBERRY SALSA:
1/2 c. Raspberries, fresh, washed and left whole
1/2 c. Sweet red pepper, chopped
2 Serrano peppers, fresh, finely minced
1/4 c. Red onion, chopped
1/2 c. Tomato, ripe, seeded and chopped
2 T. Cilantro, fresh, finely chopped
Pinch Salt

Gently combine all the salsa ingredients, being careful to leave the raspberries whole. Allow to set 1 hour.

Serve chilled with chilled shrimp.

Makes Four Servings

Salad Greens with Extravaberryraspaganza Dressing

4 Salad greens, arugula, watercress or other salad greens, portions

EXTRAVABERRYRASPAGANZA DRESSING:
1/3 c. Raspberry vinegar
1 t. Dijon mustard
Salt and pepper (to taste)
1/2 c. Olive oil

1 c. Raspberries, fresh, washed
2 T. Chives, chopped

Fresh mixed salad greens, arugula or watercress to serve four.

Whisk raspberry vinegar, Dijon mustard, salt, pepper, and olive oil together.

Arrange greens on platter or bowl. Toss with dressing and garnish with berries and chives.

Makes Four Servings

Melt butter in skillet large enough to hold chicken breasts. Add breasts and cook about 4 minutes per side until golden brown. Remove and cover to keep warm.

Sauté onion in butter in skillet over low heat until tender. Add raspberry vinegar, raise heat and cook until syrupy, stirring occasionally. Whisk in cream and chicken stock, simmer 2 minutes.

Return chicken breasts to skillet and simmer at low temperature for 5 minutes until breasts are hot. Remove breasts to platter. Add raspberries to sauce and heat for 1 minute, being careful not to break up the berries.

Pour sauce over chicken and serve with rice.

Makes Six Servings

2 lb.	Chicken breasts, boneless, skinless
2 T.	Butter
1/4 c.	Onion, finely chopped
4 T.	Raspberry vinegar
1/4 c.	Chicken stock
1/4 c.	Cream
1/2 c.	Raspberries, fresh, left whole

Rocky Mountain Berries, Berries, & More Berries

The four most popular berries are strawberries, raspberries, chokecherries, and mulberries. Two of the hotel restaurants — The Plaza in Las Vegas, New Mexico, and the Izaak Walton Inn in Essex, Montana — feature their own local berries extensively in their selections, raspberries and mulberries, respectively.

Near Las Vegas is La Cueva, which has magnificent raspberries. La Cueva is a National Historic District, and the raspberry growing heritage has resulted in raspberries that have intense flavor, due in part to the long history of their propagation and passed-down skills to bring their flavors to the fore, as well as the high altitude sun, and the controlled watering to intensify flavors.

The mulberries are native to the area of Northern Montana where the Izaak Walton is located. Mother Nature propagates these plants, and the local gatherers must compete with the black, brown, and grizzly bears for the berries. No wonder the mulberries come quite dear!

Raspberry Chimichurri

6-8	Garlic cloves, minced
1/2 c.	Cilantro, tightly packed
2 c.	Parsley, tightly packed
3 t.	Oregano, dried
2 t.	Thyme, dried
2 t.	Rosemary
2	Bay leaves
1 t.	Black peppercorns
1 t.	Red pepper, crushed
3/4 c.	Raspberry vinegar
3/4 c.	Olive oil
1/2 t.	Sale

Combine seasonings in food processor. Add raspberry vinegar, olive oil, and sale to thicken sauce.

Serve with grilled meats.

Makes About One Cup

Raspberry Flan

CARAMEL:

1/2 c.	Sugar
3 T.	Water
1 c.	Raspberries

CUSTARD:

1 c.	Orange juice
5	Eggs, lightly beaten
2	Egg yolks, lightly beaten
1/2 c.	Sugar
2 T.	Whipping cream
1 T.	Grand Marnier
1/2 t.	Vanilla

Combine sugar and water in a small heavy saucepan and cook over medium heat until thick and amber colored. Pour into individual cups or a 4- to 5-cup mold. Swirl to coat bottom, and set aside to cool. Scatter raspberries across caramel.

Whisk all ingredients together. Pour into caramel mold or cups and set into water bath, halfway up the sides.

Bake at 350-degree oven until custard is set, about 30 to 45 minutes. Cool to room temperature and refrigerate for 2 hours. Unmold and serve.

Makes Six to Eight Servings

Raspberry Margarita

Mix all ingredients in tumbler with ice and shake. Strain into martini glass with salted rim and serve with lime wedge.

Makes One Serving

1-1/2 oz.	Cuervo Silver tequila
1/2 oz.	Cointreau
3 T.	Lime juice, fresh (sweet and sour mix may be used but will produce a sweeter drink)
1 oz.	Raspberries, fresh, crushed, strained, and mixed with
1-2 T.	Sugar (to taste)

Chocolate Raspberry Torte

Preheat oven to 350 degrees. Butter and flour two 9-inch cake pans. Cream eggs, mayonnaise, and sugar until light and fluffy. Sift together dry ingredients. Mix water and vanilla, and add to creamed mixture, alternating with dry ingredients, beginning and ending with dry ingredients.

Bake in two 9-inch cake pans at 350-degree oven for 35 to 40 minutes, until center is done. Let cool completely.

Mix raspberries and sugar in heavy saucepan and reduce for 30 to 40 minutes. Cool before spreading on cake.

Carefully melt chocolate in heavy-bottomed saucepan. Whisk in cream and simmer over low heat, until syrupy.

TO ASSEMBLE CAKES: Cut the two layers in half. Place one round on cake plate and spread with raspberry filling. Repeat with two additional halves. Place final half on top and spread with ganache. Chill cake 4 hours, until ready to serve.

Makes Twelve Servings

4	Eggs
1 c.	Mayonnaise
1-3/4 c.	Sugar
3/4 c.	Cocoa powder
2 c.	Flour
1/4 t.	Baking soda
1-1/2 t.	Baking powder
1-1/3 c.	Water
1-1/2 t.	Vanilla

RASPBERRY FILLING:

1 lb.	Raspberries
2 c.	Sugar

CHOCOLATE GANACHE:

3 oz.	Semi-sweet chocolate
1/4 c.	Heavy cream

Chile Peppers

Southwestern recipes feature the use of chile peppers, with a greater variety of chiles used today than in years past. Each has a different taste and different degree of hotness, as measured by Scoville units, which is the very un-scientific measurement of how many units of water it takes to neutralize one unit of capsaicin, the heat-causing substance contained in chile peppers.

Many of the recipes feature specific kinds of chiles. Substitute as you feel inclined or as local supply dictates, but individual chiles can vary significantly in hotness. So, the chart on the next page is a *guide*.

A couple of cautions:

- The oil from chiles can burn soft tissue, so wear rubber gloves when processing chiles and do not touch your eyes!

- The chile powder referred to in the recipes is ground New Mexico red chile powder. Commercial preparations called "chili powder" often contain extra spices.

- Chipotle chiles are smoked jalapeños and are available dried or canned, and the dried are often hotter. The process of rehydrating will release their smokiness into the water or sauce. If you like it smokey, hold the water.

- Big-size chiles tend to be mild, smaller sizes tend to be hotter.

- Chiles are reputed to release endorphins and that's one reason we like them so well!

Have fun with your chile cooking!

Chile Heat Chart

2-3	*Anaheim*	The most typical, large supermarket chile. About 500 on the Scoville scale.
2-4	*Güajillo*	A Mexican dried chile. Complex flavor.
3	*Poblano*	Dried form is Ancho (3-5).
3-5	*New Mexico*	Lots of hybrids.
5-6	*Huachinango*	Large jalapeño, red.
5.5	*Jalapeño*	Dried smoked form is Chipotle.
6.5	*Fresno*	Chile Caribe is made from this.
6.5	*Güero*	Hungarian wax, other yellow chiles.
6-7	*Pasilla*	True pasilla is Mexican and is dried. California has a green pasilla which is different.
6-7	*Korean Chile*	Similar to Thai chiles, but larger and fresh.
7	*Serrano*	"Green bullets from hell", native to Mexico, less widely available in U.S.
7-8	*Rocotillo*	Flavor of Scotch Bonnet, but none of the heat.
7-8	*Thai*	Most often used dried.
8	*Cayenne*	Most familiar in powdered form, but can be found fresh, and found all over the world.
8	*Tepín*	The original wild chile. Rare. Small.
9	*Jamaican Hot*	Watch out!
9-10	*Macho*	Green. Small. And lives up to its name.
10	*Habanero*	Use sparingly. Can be 10 to 20 times hotter than a Jalapeño.
10	*Scotch Bonnet*	Acclaimed as hotest commercially available chile pepper in the world. Can be 300,000 on the Scoville scale.

The scale is not linear. It is progressive, e.g., a Scotch Bonnet can be 600 times hotter than an Anaheim!

La Posada, Albuquerque's award-winning historic hotel, was built by New Mexico native Conrad Hilton. Today, it stands as one of the finest hotels in the Southwest. Lovingly restored in 1985, the 114-room hotel retains its original style and grace while offering traditional Southwestern hospitality. Each guestroom features Spanish tile and hand-crafted furniture, plus conveniences expected by today's traveler. La Posada de Albuquerque's enchanting lobby bar, with its hand-painted murals, hand-carved beams and second-story balconies acts as the city's most popular meeting spot. Conrad's Downtown is renowned for its award-winning cuisine and personal service. La Posada offers meeting and banquet facilities including bright, comfortable hospitality suites and a beautiful Southwestern ballroom. Situated on historic Route 66, in the heart of Albuquerque, La Posada is one block from the Convention Center, just minutes from Old Town Plaza and many fine museums. Golf, tennis, and skiing are located close by.

125 Second Street NW, Albuquerque, NM / Phone: 1-505-242-9090, 1-800-777-5732, Fax: 1-505-242-8664

Albuquerque ☆ NEW MEXICO ☆ 114 Rooms

★ 1939 ★

La Posada
de Albuquerque

Gambas con Salsa de Gaspacho

1 lb.	Shrimp, 16-20, cooked, peeled, deveined

SALSA DE GASPACHO:

1	Cucumber, seeded, peeled, finely diced
1	Onion, small, finely diced
4	Jalapeños, finely diced
3	Tomatoes, seeded, finely diced
8 T.	Olive oil
4 T.	Red wine vinegar
1 T.	Cilantro, chopped
1	Lime, squeezed

Mix shrimp with salsa and put in a container, marinate overnight. Salt to taste.

Serve with an ice cold Tecate (beer).

Makes Two to Four Servings

Jicama con Alcaparras (Capers)

1	Jícama, peeled and diced
4 T.	Olive oil
1 T.	Lemon juice
1 T.	Orange juice
1/2 T.	Onion, chopped
2 T.	Capers
Pinch	Cilantro, chopped
Pinch	Jalapeño, chopped
Pinch	Red bell pepper, diced
	Salt and pepper (to taste)

Mix all ingredients.

Makes Two Servings

Alcachofas con Gambas y Jamon

Melt butter, and sauté garlic and shallots. Add artichokes, shrimp, and ham, and cook until tender (about 5 minutes). Add sherry, red pepper, and seasonings. Cook until thoroughly heated. Serve hot.

Makes One Serving

1 t.	Butter
1/4 t.	Garlic
1/4 t.	Shallots
2	Artichoke hearts, halved
4	Shrimp
Pinch	Ham, julienne
2 t.	Sherry
2 t.	Red pepper, diced
Pinch	Chipotle pepper
1 t.	Cilantro, chopped

Vieriras al Vino Blanco

Melt butter, and sauté garlic, shallots, peppers, jalapeños, and carrots. Add scallops, white wine, sherry, and cook until tender (about 5 to 10 minutes). Serve hot, sprinkle with cilantro and lime.

Makes One Serving

1 t.	Butter
1/4 t.	Garlic
1/4 t.	Shallots
Pinch	Red bell pepper
Pinch	Jalapeño, chopped
Pinch	Carrots, julienne
4	Bay scallops
1 T.	White wine
1 T.	Sherry
Pinch	Cilantro
Squeeze	Lime

Sopa de Tortilla

Melt butter, sauté garlic, onion, celery, and carrots until tender. Add tomatoes, jalapeños, chicken stock, cilantro, and lime juice. Cook until boiling point, then reduce heat and simmer for 30 minutes.

Serve with fried tortilla strips.

Makes Six to Eight Servings

4 T.	Butter
6	Garlic cloves, minced
1	Onion, diced
1/2 c.	Celery, diced
1	Carrot, diced
6	Tomatoes, diced
2	Jalapeños, chopped
1 gal.	Chicken stock
1/2 c.	Cilantro, chopped
3	Limes, juice
	Tortilla strips, fried

Chuleta de Cordero

12	Lamb chops, frenched
16 - 20	Shrimp, peeled and deveined

ROSEMARY, SERRANO, AND BUTTER:

1/4 c.	Lime juice
1/8 t.	Salt
1/8 t.	Garlic, fresh
1 t.	Rosemary, ground
3	Serranos, minced
1 T.	Cilantro, chopped
8 oz.	Butter, softened

Broil lamb chops and shrimp, then put rosemary, serrano, and butter over the top, melt and serve.

Makes Six Servings

Mix garlic, lime juice, salt, rosemary, serranos, cilantro, and butter. Keep at room temperature. Set aside.

Pechuga de Pollo Borracho

2	Chicken breasts, 8 oz., skinless and boneless
1 t.	Olive oil
1/4 t.	Shallots
1/4 t.	Garlic
Pinch	Sage
Pinch	Cumin
1 t.	Capers
1 t.	Tomatoes, sun-dried
1 T.	Prosciutto ham strips, diced
1 oz.	Tequila
4 oz.	Chicken stock
1 oz.	Heavy cream
	Salt and pepper (to taste)
	Cilantro leaves

Flour chicken breasts and sauté in olive oil until browned. Add shallots, garlic, sage, cumin, capers, tomatoes, and proscuitto. Sauté until tender. Add tequila, chicken stock, heavy cream, cook until sauce reduces to a thick sauce. Remove breasts and pour sauce over chicken breasts. Serve hot.

Garnish with cilantro leaves.

Makes Two Servings

Flan de Cafe

Place in saucepan and heat on high flame until sugar melts (careful not to burn). Remove when caramel color.

Mix milk, sugar, vanilla extract, instant coffee, eggs, and egg yolks thoroughly. Put caramel into 6 dessert cups. Pour custard mixture on top of the caramel in the cups. Place cups in a pan with water and cover. Bake at 375 degrees for 1 to 1-1/2 hours.

Makes Six Servings

CARAMEL:
3/4 c.	Sugar

THE CUSTARD:
1 qt.	Milk
1/2 c.	Sugar
1/2 t.	Vanilla extract
2 T.	Instant coffee
4	Whole eggs
2	Egg yolks

La Po-Soda

Mix all ingredients. Serve over ice and garnish with lime.

Makes One Serving

1 oz.	Tequila or rum
6 oz.	Limeade
Splash	Soda

Coco-Loco

Blend all ingredients.

Makes One Serving

4 oz.	Coconut milk
4 oz.	Lime juice, fresh
2 oz.	Rum

Steps from Santa Fe's celebrated plaza is the refined Hotel St. Francis. Built in 1924, the hotel is located on the same site as its fire-damaged 19th-century predecessor. The hotel is now acclaimed for its authentic restoration and preservation. The St. Francis' spacious lobby and outdoor veranda are popular spots for afternoon tea, cordials, and scrumptious housemade desserts. Each room and suite is unique with cherry-wood and marble furnishings, brass or iron beds, and porcelain pedestal sinks. Many have inspiring mountain views. "On Water" Restaurant is a local favorite and one of Santa Fe's finest. Its distinctive menu changes weekly and offers the finest Rocky Mountain cuisine. The St. Francis provides guests an elegant alternative in Santa Fe, the 380-year-old "city different," that is convenient to Santa Fe's shopping, art galleries, museums, and historic sites. Downhill and cross-country skiing, and hiking trails can be found nearby. The St. Francis is the perfect location to enjoy Indian Market or Opera.

210 Don Gaspar Ave., Santa Fe, NM / Phone: 1-505-983-5700, 1-800-529-5700, Fax: 1-505-989-7690

Santa Fe ✶ NEW MEXICO ✶ 82 Rooms

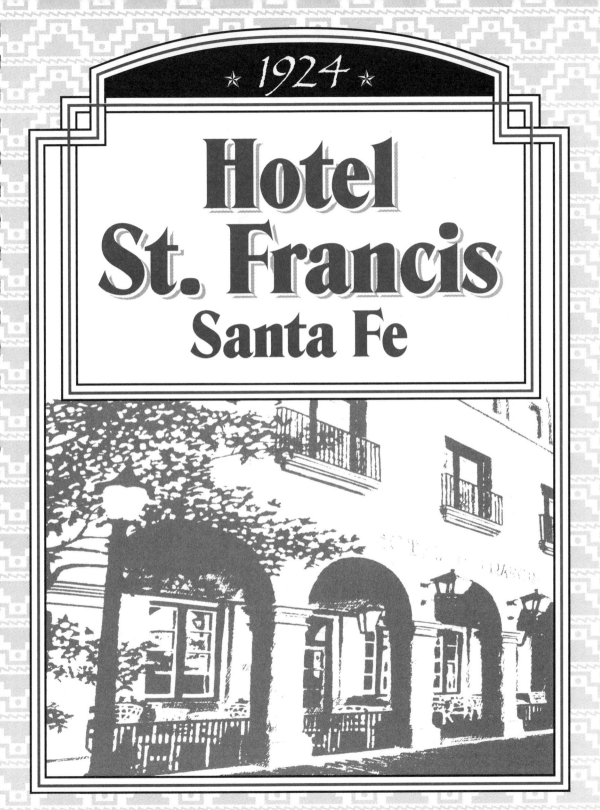

* 1924 *

Hotel
St. Francis
Santa Fe

Peppery Lentil Soup

1   Onion, medium, peeled and coarsely chopped
1   Carrot, coarsely chopped
1   Bell pepper, coarsely chopped
1 T.   Garlic, minced
2 c.   Lentils, cooked and drained (reserving the water)
1   Tomatoes, large can, chopped
1/2 T.   Cayenne
1/2 T.   Ground black pepper, ground white pepper, New Mexico red chili powder (each)
1 T.   Cumin
     Salt and pepper (to taste)

In large pot, sauté onion, carrot, bell pepper, and garlic. Add remaining ingredients and simmer, using the lentil water to achieve the desired thickness.

Serve hot or cold, garnished with cilantro and creme fraiche.

Makes Four Servings

Mushroom Wild Rice Pancakes

2 c.   Wild rice, cooked
1   Onion, large, finely diced
3   Garlic cloves, minced
1/2 t.   Oregano, sage, basil, thyme (each)
6 T.   Butter
2 T.   Olive oil
1/2 lb.   White mushrooms, chopped
10   Shitake mushrooms, sliced
3 T.   Soy sauce
1/4 c.   Parsley, minced
5   Eggs, separated
1/2-3/4 c.   All purpose flour
1/2 lb.   Parmesan, grated

In 2 T. of butter, sauté onion, garlic, and herbs, until onion is transparent. Add cooked wild rice and set aside.

In remaining butter and olive oil, sauté mushrooms until done, and add to rice mixture. Add soy sauce and parsley.

Beat egg whites until they form stiff peaks, set aside. Beat egg yolks until light yellow. Add flour and cheese to egg yolks. Gently blend with rice mixture. Fold in egg whites. Cook on medium-hot, greased griddle.

Excellent with Quinces with Young Chicken.

Makes Two Servings

Preheat oven to 400 degrees. Rinse chicken and livers under cold water; pat dry. Sprinkle inside of chicken with salt and pepper; put livers in cavity. Brush with clarified butter. Roast in oven for approximately 30 minutes. Chicken should be half cooked, but still pink. Remove from oven and cool. When cool enough to touch, remove skin. Remove livers and reserve. Drain off chicken fat and reserve. Bone chicken and set aside.

Blanch quince wedges in boiling water for 30 seconds; shock in ice water. Pat dry and reserve.

In skillet over medium heat, sauté onion and liver in rendered chicken fat until onions are transparent. Drain off and reserve chicken fat.

In a bowl, combine flour and wine; add chicken stock and mix until smooth.

Layer quinces in bottom of baking pan. Cover with onions and livers. Pour thickened chicken stock over layers. Next, layer all chicken meat on top. Brush chicken with reserved chicken fat. Return to oven and bake until golden and done, approximately 10 more minutes. Remove from oven and serve.

Makes Two Servings

1	Chicken, whole, 3 lb.
4-6	Chicken livers
1/4 c.	Butter, unsalted, clarified
3	Quinces, large, peeled, cored, and sliced into wedges
1/2 c.	Onion, finely minced
2 T.	Flour
1/2 c.	White wine
1 c.	Chicken stock
	Salt and pepper (to taste)

Pickled Fennel

2	Fennel, large bunches, sliced crosswise, evenly
1/4 c.	Sugar
4	Bay leaves
4 c.	White wine vinegar
1/2 c.	Water
1/4 t.	Salt, mustard seed, dill weed (each)
1 T.	Red chili, crushed
1 T.	Dill seed
2	Garlic cloves, minced

Cook fennel in boiling water. Leave crunchy; shock in ice water. Drain and set aside with bay leaves.

Mix remaining ingredients in saucepan and heat until sugar and salt are dissolved.

Pack fennel and bay leaves in jar. Pour liquid over fennel, making sure all is covered with liquid. Allow to cool; place lid on jar and refrigerate.

The pickled fennel is ready to serve in 48 hours. If kept refrigerated, it will remain good up to one week.

Makes Two Servings

Bleu Cheese Cake

4 oz.	Bleu cheese
4 T.	Butter, softened
8 oz.	Cream cheese
6	Eggs
5 T.	Crème fraiche
	Salt and pepper (to taste)

Heat oven to 350 degrees. Combine all ingredients in food processor until smooth. Place in 8-inch spring form pan. Bake in bain marie (water bath) for approximately 30 minutes or until set. Remove from oven and allow to cool.

Remove from pan and serve garnished with chopped chives and accompanied by water crackers or crusty bread.

Makes Eight Servings

Carrot Cake

Heat oven to 350 degrees. Grease and flour the sides and bottom of 3 round layer pans. Cut circle of wax paper for bottom of each pan and insert. Set aside.

Sift together flour, cinnamon, soda, and salt. Beat oil, eggs, and sugar until light. Stir in carrots. Next stir in sifted dry ingredients and finally, stir in the chopped walnuts.

Pour batter into prepared pans. Bake about 30 minutes or until sides of cake pull away from pan.

Set aside and cool. Remove from pans when still warm. Remove wax paper circles from bottom of layers.

Cream butter and cream cheese. Mix in powdered sugar; beat until smooth. Add vanilla; beat until completely incorporated.

This makes enough frosting to frost between the layers and cover the exterior of the cake with medium coverage.

Makes One Cake

2 c.+2 T.	All purpose flour
1-1/2 t.	Baking soda
2 c.	Sugar
Pinch	Salt
2 t.	Cinnamon
1-1/2 T.	Oil
6	Eggs
3-1/2 c.	Carrots, finely grated
1/2 c.	Black walnuts, chopped

CREAM CHEESE FROSTING:

1 box	Powdered sugar
1/4 lb.	Butter, softened
8 oz.	Cream cheese
1 t.	Vanilla

The romantic charm of the Southwest comes to life at The Taos Inn. Made up of several adobe houses dating from the 1800s, the Inn's two-story lobby, whose fountain replaces an old town well, acts as the community's living room. Its 39 guestrooms are individually furnished with hand-crafted Southwestern furniture, pueblo-style fireplaces, hand-loomed bedspreads, and antiques, as well as the more modern conveniences of telephones, private baths, and cable television. The outdoor pool is popular in the summer and the greenhouse-Jacuzzi is used year-round. Doc Martin's Restaurant is known for innovative Rocky Mountain and Northern New Mexican cuisines and its wine list has received an "Award of Excellence" from the **Wine Spectator**. The intimate Adobe Bar features Taos' best international beer, margaritas, espresso menu, and live entertainment.

The Taos Inn is only steps from historic Taos Plaza, art galleries, museums, shops, and restaurants. Visitors enjoy the Inn's "Meet-the-Artist" Series, Taos Pueblo, skiing, Rio Grande Gorge, St. Francisco de Asis Church, and many tri-cultural events.

125 Paseo del Pueblo Norte, Taos, NM / Phone: 1-505-758-2233, 1-800-TAOS INN, Fax: 1-505-758-5776

Taos ✴ NEW MEXICO ✴ 39 Rooms

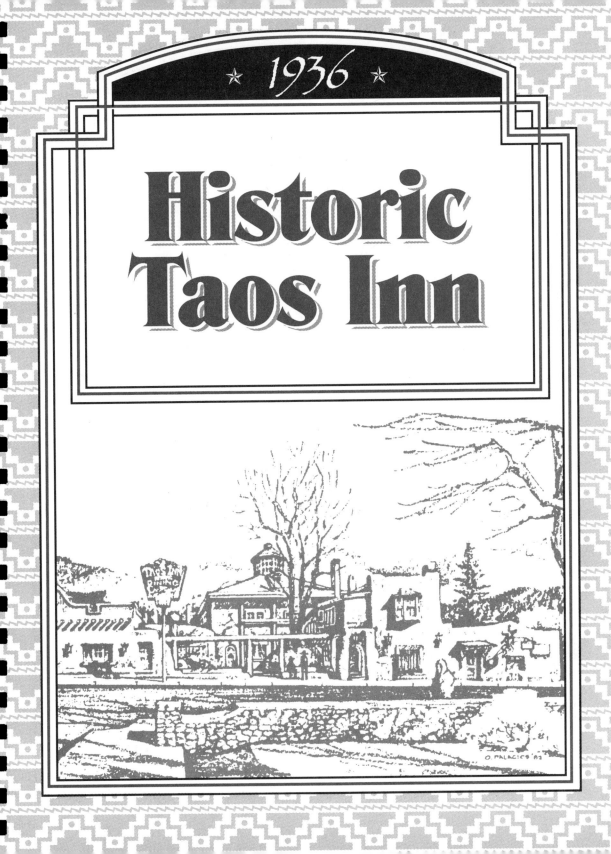

⋆ 1936 ⋆

Historic
Taos Inn

Guacamole

12	Avocados, *ripe*
1/2	Yellow onion, *diced*
3	Jalapeños, *finely chopped*
1/2 c.	Lemon juice
	Salt (*to taste*)
3	Garlic cloves, *minced*
1	Tomato, *diced*

Cut avocados in half, remove pit, and scoop meat out of skin. Dice yellow onion and tomato in 1/4-inch pieces. Place jalapeños and garlic in food processor, pulse until coarsely chopped. Mix all ingredients thoroughly.

NOTE: NO NOT MIX TOO LONG! You are making guacamole, not baby food.

To Store: Squeeze lemon or lime juice over guacamole to prevent oxidation.

Makes Ten to Twelve Servings

Pheasant Salad with Cranberry Vinaigrette

8	Pheasant breasts, *cooked, skinless, julienne*
1 qt.	Mixed greens
2	Apples, *sliced*
1	Red onion, *sliced*
4	Potatoes, *boiled, peeled and sliced*
1/4 c.	Cashews

VINAIGRETTE:

1-1/2 c.	Dried cranberries
2 c.	Apple juice
1 c.	Cranberry juice
3	Shallots, *medium, minced*
2 c.	Rice wine vinegar
1-1/2 c.	Olive oil (*approximately*)
8	Tomato wedges
8	Cucumber, *sliced or whole*

Toss pheasant breasts, greens, apples, red onion, potatoes, and cashews in vinaigrette.

Place a tomato wedge and cucumber on plate and place mixture in high pile on plate.

Makes Eight Servings

Bar Salsa

Finely chop (or purée in food processor) jalapeños and cilantro. Purée tomatoes. Combine all ingredients and chill.

Makes One Gallon

1	Tomatoes, whole, peeled (large can)
4	Garlic cloves, minced
	Salt (to taste)
2 t.	Chile pequin
1	Cilantro, fresh bunch, chopped
1	Green onion, bunch, chopped

Sopaipillas (Southwestern Fried Bread)

In a bowl, whisk together the flours, sugar, and salt. In a small saucepan, heat the milk and butter over moderately low heat, stirring, until the butter is melted and mixture is just warm. Remove the pan from heat. Sprinkle the yeast over the milk mixture and proof it for 10 minutes, or until it is foamy. In an electric mixer fitted with the dough hook, beat the milk mixture with half the flour mixture on low speed until the mixture is combined and beat in the remaining flour mixture, beating until the mixture forms a dough. (The dough will be slightly sticky.)

Transfer the dough to a lightly oiled bowl, turn dough to coat it with the oil, and let it rise, covered with a kitchen towel in a warm place for 1 hour. Turn the dough out onto a lightly floured surface, roll it out 1/4-inch thick, and let it rise, covered with the towel, for 30 minutes more. In a small saucepan, heat the honey and cinnamon, whisking until it is warm.

Cut the dough with a sharp knife into 3-inch squares or triangles and cover the squares with a dampened kitchen towel. In a kettle, heat 2 inches of the oil until it is 375 degrees on a deep-fat thermometer and fry the squares, a few at a time, turning them, for 1 minute, or until they are puffed and golden brown, transferring them as they are fried to paper towels to drain. Serve warm with the cinnamon honey.

1 c.+2 T.	Whole wheat flour
1 c.+2 T.	All purpose flour
1 t.	Sugar
1/2 t.	Salt
1 c.	Milk
2 T.	Butter, unsalted
1 t.	Active dry yeast
1/2 c.	Honey
1/2 t.	Cinnamon
	Vegetable oil
	Flour

Makes 12 Servings

Chili Rellenos with Smoked Duck, Pinon & Jack Cheese

PREPARE THE FILLING:

3	Smoked duck breasts, medium sized
1/2 c.	Piñon nuts, roasted
4 c.	Jack cheese, grated
	Vegetable oil

Sauté duck breasts in hot oil. Sauté until medium rare. Remove from pan, skin, and julienne. Mix with remaining ingredients. Set aside, refrigerate.

PREPARE ANAHEIM CHILES:

20-22	Anaheim chiles, fresh

Roast the whole chiles until they blister. This can be done on a grill, in the oven, or in a hot pan. Place the chiles in a bowl and cover with plastic wrap to steam themselves for about 20 minutes. After steaming, remove skins. Remove stem and seeds by pulling the stem out, seeds will come with it. Rinse out remaining seeds from inside of the chile, taking care not to break up the whole chile.

Stuff the chiles with the filling, retain the shape of the chile.

PREPARE RED CHILE:

2	Onion, medium, quartered
3	Garlic cloves
2 qts.	Water
1/4 c.	Chile powder
1 T.	Flour
2 T.	Olive oil

Boil onions and garlic cloves in water about 45 minutes. Strain, retaining the broth. In a hot pan, toast the chile powder until it turns three shades darker red. Add the flour and olive oil and whisk over heat to make a roux. Whisk in the onion broth gradually until mixture reaches liquid thickness (not watery). Bring to a boil, simmer and reduce for 25 minutes.

PREPARE RELLENO MERINGUE:

20	Eggs, separated
1/4 c.	Flour

Beat the egg whites until stiff but not dry. Whisk the flour into the egg yolks until smooth. Fold the egg whites into yolk mixture. Place the bowl with meringue mixture over an ice bath.

TO ASSEMBLE:

	Stuffed peppers
	Meringue
2 c.	Flour
	Vegetable oil

Gently dredge stuffed pepper in flour; dip into meringue being sure to cover the entire chile. Gently lower the chile into the fryer or a fry pan with 1/4-inch of hot oil. Fry until first side is golden brown. Carefully turn over the chile, and fry until second side is golden brown. Gently remove chile from frying pan. Place on serving dish. Spoon the red chile over the rellenos and serve.

Makes Six Servings

Grilled Buffalo Steak with Bing Cherry Demi-Glace

Clean and tenderize buffalo steaks. Simmer bing cherries and red wine until it is reduced in half. Add chopped thyme and beef stock. Reduce this combination to one-third of original mixture, let cool and brush on buffalo steaks while grilling.

4	Buffalo, New York Strip portion
4 to 6 c.	Bing cherries
3 c.	Red wine
1 T.	Thyme
6 c.	Beef stock

Makes Four Servings

Doc Martin's Award-Winning Green Chile

"This green chile has become world famous. New Mexicans drive two hours to the Inn just for the green chile."

In a small heavy skillet, cook 4T. of butter and 1/4 c. of flour over moderately low heat, stirring for 3 minutes and reserve this roux.

In a heavy kettle, heat the oil over moderate heat until it is hot but not smoking, add the ground meats and cubed chuck, stirring to break up lumps. Cook until meat is no longer pink and transfer with slotted spoon to a bowl. In remaining fat plus 3 T. butter, cook the onion and garlic over moderate low heat, stirring until onion is soft, add the coriander, parsley, Tabasco, oregano, cumin, and black pepper. Add remaining 2 T. flour and cook stirring, for 3 minutes. Add meat, broth, beer, chiles, and tomato. Bring to a boil, stirring. Stir in reserved roux, stirring until well mixed. Simmer the chile, stirring occasionally, about 1 hour.

The chile improves if made one day ahead, allowed to cool completely, uncovered, kept covered and chilled, and reheated.

Serve the chile topped with the freshly grated, sharp Cheddar and Monterey Jack cheeses, chopped lettuce, and chopped tomatoes and serve *sopaipillas* separately.

7 T.	Butter, unsalted
1/4 c.+2 T.	Flour
1 T.	Oil, vegetable
1/2 lb.	Ground beef, ground pork
1/2 lb.	Chuck roast (cut in 1/2-inch cubes)
1	Onion, large, finely chopped
3	Garlic cloves, minced
1/3 c.	Coriander, fresh, chopped
1 T.	Parsley, fresh, chopped
2 t.	Tabasco
1 t.	Oregano, dried, crumbled
2 t.	Cumin, ground
1/2 t.	Black pepper
3 c.	Chicken or beef stock
12 oz.	Mexican light beer
2 lbs.	Green chiles, seeded, diced, peeled
1	Tomato, diced

Makes Four to Six Servings

Southwestern Corn Soup

5	Russet (baking) potatoes
2	Sweet potatoes (~ 1 lb.)
1-1/2 T.	Vegetable oil
3	White onions, medium, chopped fine
1/4 c.	Garlic, minced
1/2 c.	Celery, chopped fine
1/2 c.	Green chiles, mild, chopped
1	Red and green bell pepper, (each), chopped fine
1-1/2 c.	Corn kernels, fresh or frozen
1 T.	Oregano, dried, crumbled
1/2 T.	Basil, dried, crumbled
1 T.	Cumin, ground
1/2 c.	Dry white wine
1/2 c.	Coriander leaves, fresh, finely chopped
	Salt (to taste)

In a large saucepan, combine the baking potatoes and sweet potatoes, both peeled and cut into 1/2-inch cubes, with enough cold water to cover them by 1 inch. Simmer, uncovered, for 30 minutes, or until they are tender, and remove the pan from the heat.

In a kettle, heat the oil over moderately high heat, until it is hot, but not smoking, and in it cook the onions, garlic, celery, chiles, bell peppers, corn, oregano, basil, and cumin, stirring occasionally, until onions are softened and vegetables begin to brown. Add the wine, cook the mixture, scraping up the brown bits, for 1 minute, and add potatoes with the cooking liquid and if necessary enough water to cover the vegetables by 1 inch.

Simmer the chowder, uncovered, stirring occasionally, for 40 minutes and stir in coriander and salt to taste.

Makes Six to Ten Servings

Papas y Chiles

18	Red potatoes, small (~ 2-inch diameter)
2 T.	Butter, unsalted
2 c.	Beef and pork green chili (see recipe on previous page)
1 c.	Sharp cheddar cheese, freshly grated
1 c.	Monterey Jack cheese, freshly grated
	Sour cream
	Scallion greens, chopped
	Flour tortillas, warm

In a large saucepan of salted, gently boiling water, cook the potatoes for 15 minutes or until they are tender, drain them, and cut in half. Preheat the broiler. In a large, heavy cast iron skillet, heat the butter over moderately high heat until the foam subsides, in it brown the potatoes, seasoned with salt and pepper, until they are slightly crusted, and transfer them to a flameproof serving dish. Spoon the green chili over the potatoes, sprinkle the potatoes with the cheeses, and broil the mixture about 4 inches from the heat for 2 minutes, or until the cheeses are melted.

Serve the chiles topped with the sour cream and scallions and serve the tortillas separately.

Makes Six Servings

Venison Tamales with Guajillo Chile Sauce

Place venison, onion, garlic, and oregano in large stock pot and fill with water. Bring to a boil, and reduce to simmer, cook until meat can easily be pulled apart. Strain broth and set aside. Pull meat apart with two forks. Cover with chile sauce. Marinate overnight.

Rinse chiles with cold water, pat dry, remove stems, seeds, and veins. Place in large pot. Cover with venison stock. Bring to boil, reduce heat and simmer 2 to 3 hours until chiles are soft. Add seasonings and simmer another 10 minutes.

Put in blender and blend as smooth as possible. Pour sauce through strainer.

In large mixing bowl, combine masa harina and salt. Make well in center of masa. Put lard in well. Pour stock, a little at a time, into well as you combine by hand, until well mixed. Add goat cheese, corn, piñon nuts, and oregano. Mix well. Refrigerate overnight. Pull apart and place the oven-dried corn husks in a large container. Cover with hot water. Soak overnight.

Pat corn husks dry. Spread corn husks flat. Place 3 T. masa in center of each and press into a square. Then spread all the way to the sides and top edge, leaving about 2 inches at the bottom end uncovered. Place 3 T. of meat mixture in center of masa. Fold over one side, then the other to overlap. Fold up bottom. Place fold down in steamer. Steam tamales 1 hour.

Serve with chile sauce.

Makes Eight to Ten Servings

8 lb.	Venison, 1-inch cubes
1	White onion, quartered
6	Garlic cloves
3	Oregano sprigs
	Water

CHILE SAUCE:

2-3 lbs.	Güajillo chiles (or dry red chiles)
1/4 c.	Garlic, minced
2 T.	Cumin
1 T.	Oregano, Mexican, fresh chopped
	Venison broth

MASA:

3 lb.	Masa harina (dough)
1 lb.	Lard
1 T.	Salt
5 c.	Venison broth, lukewarm
1 c.	Corn, fresh
11 oz.	Goat cheese
1/2 c.	Piñon nuts, roasted
1 T.	Oregano, Mexican, fresh chopped
30	Corn husks

Biscotti

1 c.	Sugar
1/2 c.	Butter, melted
2 T.	Anise seeds
2 T.	Anisette or other anise liqueur
4-1/2 t.	Bourbon
1 c.	Almonds, coarsely chopped
3	Eggs, large
2-3/4 c.	All purpose flour
1-1/2 t.	Baking powder

In a bowl, mix sugar, butter, anise seeds, anise liqueur, bourbon, almonds, and eggs. Beat to blend. In another bowl, mix together flour and baking powder. Add dry ingredients to butter mixture and blend thoroughly. Shape dough into two long loaves (approximately 3-inches wide.) Cover and let rest at room temperature for 30 minutes. Bake until light brown in 375-degree oven about 7 to 8 minutes. After baking, slice diagonally into 3/4-inch slices and arrange cut side up on baking sheet. Lightly toast slices in oven (approximately 3 minutes).

Makes Three Dozen Cookies

Adobe Bar Classic Margarita

1 oz.	Cuervo Gold tequila
1-1/2 oz.	Sweet and Sour mix
1/4 oz.	Cointreau
Splash	Lime juice, fresh

Shake all ingredients with ice in cocktail shaker. Pour into Margarita glass.

Makes One Serving

Liquid Refreshments

The Rocky Mountain West is associated with the free-drinking saloons found in gold camps, cow towns, and towns and cities all along the frontier. At first the frontier imported whiskey, wine, port, sherries, and bitters. Soon, the Rockies got their stills and breweries going full-time and importation of whiskey and beer from the east dropped off. The imported wines did not. Just like oysters, fine wines, ports and sherries were de-rigeur for any fine meal. Special wine stores are not a late twentieth-century device; almost every significant frontier city and gold camp of the second half of the 1800s had a store featuring wine. Favorites were the wines of Bordeaux.

Perhaps the most famous frontier whiskey was "Taos Lightning". With demand for whiskey high, a restricted supply from the East, and no constraints on the purchase of a still, local distilleries sprang up. As New Mexico was part of Mexico up until 1846, many stills were set-up there as the Mexican government was not anti-whiskey. Up to five distilleries are reported to have operated in the Taos area. They did not last the century, but Taos Lightning and the folklore of the frontier certainly have.

Breweries were common in almost all settlements of the West. The large number of these breweries was due to the fact that beers did not travel or age well. Once made, they were consumed locally. As Dana Vaillancourt, Cultural Resourcers Manager of Deadwood relates:

> "Prior to 1873 and pasteurization, light beers went bad after three or four days, while stouts, ports, and ales with higher alcoholic content could be depended to last longer. Adolphus Busch started pasteurizing in 1873, and so his beers could be shipped nationally in bottles. This is a key consideration, allowing you to take a bottle home to drink without being tied to the local brew at the local saloon. Also, you did not always drink the local water. Ginger ale was also popular and was felt to have medicinal qualities. Another interesting tidbit is that small champagne bottles are often found in excavations near Western brothels. In 1878, the cost for a dozen bottles of St. Louis lager, in Deadwood, South Dakota, was $4.00."

For more on "potables" in the west, see the book entitled *Bottles on the Western Frontier*, by Rex L. Wilson, University of Arizona Press.

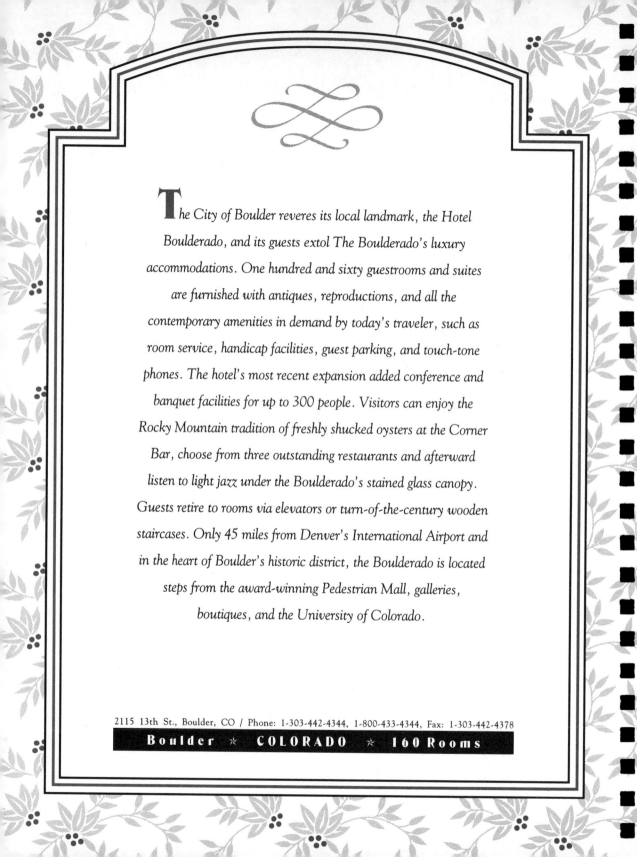

The City of Boulder reveres its local landmark, the Hotel Boulderado, and its guests extol The Boulderado's luxury accommodations. One hundred and sixty guestrooms and suites are furnished with antiques, reproductions, and all the contemporary amenities in demand by today's traveler, such as room service, handicap facilities, guest parking, and touch-tone phones. The hotel's most recent expansion added conference and banquet facilities for up to 300 people. Visitors can enjoy the Rocky Mountain tradition of freshly shucked oysters at the Corner Bar, choose from three outstanding restaurants and afterward listen to light jazz under the Boulderado's stained glass canopy. Guests retire to rooms via elevators or turn-of-the-century wooden staircases. Only 45 miles from Denver's International Airport and in the heart of Boulder's historic district, the Boulderado is located steps from the award-winning Pedestrian Mall, galleries, boutiques, and the University of Colorado.

2115 13th St., Boulder, CO / Phone: 1-303-442-4344, 1-800-433-4344, Fax: 1-303-442-4378

Boulder ✶ COLORADO ✶ 160 Rooms

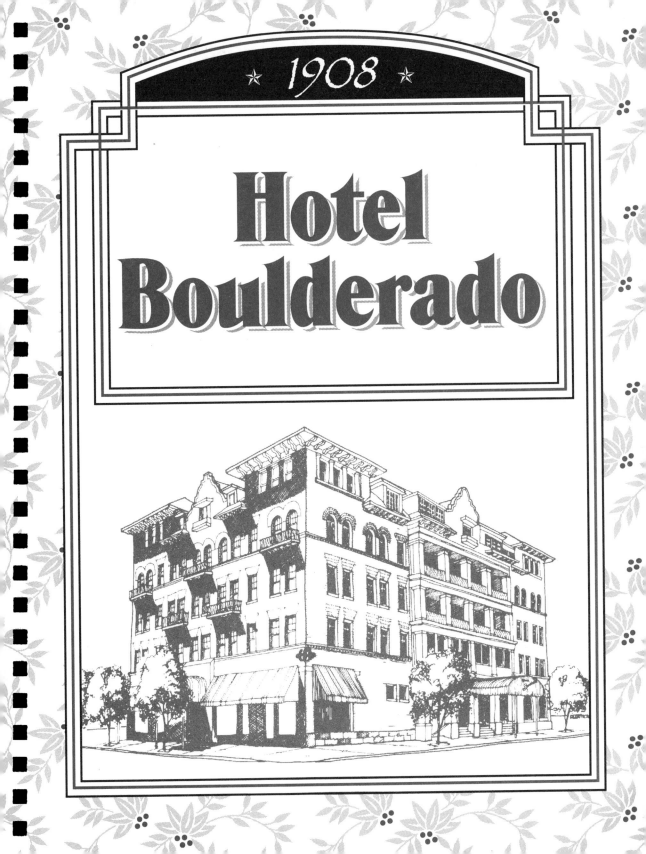

✴ 1908 ✴

Hotel Boulderado

Crunchy Salad

1 lb. Vegetables of choice

MIX MARINADE:
1/2 c. Olive oil
1/4 c. Red wine vinegar
2 T. Basil, fresh, chopped
1 Garlic clove, minced
1 T. Sesame oil
1 T. Soy sauce
Salt, pepper, and tabasco
(to taste)
Pinch Sugar

Cut up one pound (total) of the following vegetables or substitute your favorites:

Jícama	Broccoli	Zucchini
Carrots	Radishes	Red Onion
Celery	Yellow Squash	Cauliflower

Marinate the vegetables, stirring frequently, for 1/2 hour in the refrigerator. May be garnished with your choice of parmesan cheese, chopped jalapeños, sunflower seeds, sesame seeds, etc.

Makes Four to Six Servings

Grilled Chicken & Romaine Salad with Honey-Soy Dressing

4 Chicken breasts, skinless
2 Romaine lettuce, heads, chopped, washed and drained
1/2 c. Almonds, toasted, sliced
4 Scallions, sliced
1 can Crispy Lo Mein noodles

Put chicken breast on to grill. Meanwhile, toss romaine with dressing, almonds, and scallions. Divide among 4 large, chilled plates. Sprinkle with Lo Mein noodles. When chicken breasts are done, slice into thin strips, arrange on top of salad, and serve.

HONEY-SOY DRESSING:
1 T. Soy sauce
1 t. Dijon mustard
2 T. Champagne vinegar
1 T. Honey
1/4 t. Sesame oil
1/2 c. Peanut or vegetable oil

Whisk all ingredients together in stainless steel bowl. This will need to be whisked again before using.

Makes Four Servings

Mix soy sauce, sherry, ginger, garlic and sesame oil for marinade. Add the steak and marinate for 15 minutes. Heat a large wok or skillet, and add 2 T. peanut oil.

Drain beef, reserving the marinade, and stir-fry the beef for 1 minute in peanut oil. Remove beef from the wok, and add 1 T. peanut oil to the wok and stir-fry the vegetables for 1 minute. Add the beef and marinade, season with salt and pepper, and serve over steamed white rice.

Makes Four Servings

1 lb.	Flank steak, sliced thinly across the grain
2 T.	Soy sauce
2 T.	Dry sherry
1 T.	Ginger, fresh, minced
1 t.	Garlic, minced
1 t.	Sesame oil
3 T.	Peanut oil
1	Yellow onion, large, julienned
1	Red bell pepper, julienned
1	Green bell pepper, julienned
	Salt and pepper (to taste)

The Chinese Influence

The Chinese emigrated to the frontier for jobs in railroad construction, mining, and service industries. Such service also included cooking at area ranches, in addition to having in-town noodle shops and restaurants. From its early, formative years, Rocky Mountain cuisine was influenced by Chinese techniques, such as stir-fry; by ingredients, such as wontons; and by flavorings, such as soy sauce, sesame, and ginger. This merger is very typical of Rocky Mountain cuisine which has long drawn on the multiple cultures of the region — Native American to recent Hmong Laotian tribespeople. The cuisine is enrichened by this ethnic stew.

Red Chile Sauce

4 oz.	Vegetable oil
2 lbs.	Onions, sliced
1/4 c.	Garlic, minced
7 c.	Red chile purée, prepared (Güajillo chile)
2 gal.	Water
3 T.	Oregano
3 T.	Cumin
1-1/2 c.	Tomato paste
6 oz.	Chicken base
1-1/4 c.	Corn starch to thicken
1-1/4 c.	Water (combine with corn starch)

Sauté onions and garlic in oil until soft. Add Güajillo chile purée and cook for 5 minutes. Add remaining ingredients, except corn starch and water, and bring to a boil. Reduce heat and simmer for 20 minutes. Thicken with corn starch and water. Cook for 5 minutes more and strain.

Store sauce in suitable plastic container. Let it cool down, cover, refrigerate until needed.

Makes 2.5 Gallons

Pork Tenderloin with Ancho/Pomegranate Sauce

2 lb.	Pork tenderloin

SAUCE:

1/4 c.	Ancho chili purée
1 c.	Pure pomegranate juice
1/2 c.	Veal or chicken stock
	Salt and pepper (to taste)

BLACK BEAN SALSA:

1/4 c.	Black beans, cooked
1/4 c.	Corn kernels
1/4 c.	Red bell pepper, diced
1/4 c.	Anaheim pepper (or any slightly hot pepper)
3 T.	Cilantro, fresh, chopped
	Salt and pepper (to taste)

Mix Ancho chili purée, pomegranate juice, and stock. Salt and pepper to taste.

Combine black beans, corn, red pepper, anaheim pepper, and cilantro. Salt and pepper to taste. Chill.

Grill pork tenderloin to desired temperature, served fanned on ancho/pomegranate sauce and garnish with black bean salsa.

Makes Six to Eight Servings

Tournedos Chipotle

Cut the beef into eight 2-oz. portions, coat with the molasses, and sprinkle with the chili powder (and some salt and pepper to taste). This needs to be done at least 3 hours before cooking.

Heat oil in deep sauté pan, add the garlic and light brown. Next add the vinegar and cilantro. Pour in the demi-glace, bring to a boil and allow to reduce by one-quarter.

Charbroil beef over very hot coals to desired temperature. (Please, rare or medium rare, at most!)

TO SERVE: Two tournedos per serving and cover with sauce. Serve with your favorite potatoes and veggies.

Makes Four Servings

1 lb.	Beef tenderloin (with all fat and silver skin removed)
4 oz.	Blackstrap molasses
2 T.	Dark chili powder (the darker and richer the better)

SAUCE:

2 T.	Extra virgin olive oil
2 T.	Garlic, fresh, minced
2 T.	Balsamic vinegar
1 T.	Cilantro, fresh, coarsely chopped
10 oz.	Veal demi-glace (fluid oz.)
2 oz.	Chipotle peppers, diced (canned are easier than smoking your own)

Banana-Strawberry Breakfast Smoothie

Combine all ingredients in blender.

Makes Two Servings

1 c.	Ice cubes
1/2 c.	Orange juice
1 c.	Yogurt
1	Banana, peeled
1/2 pt.	Strawberries, washed, steamed
1/2 c.	Honey

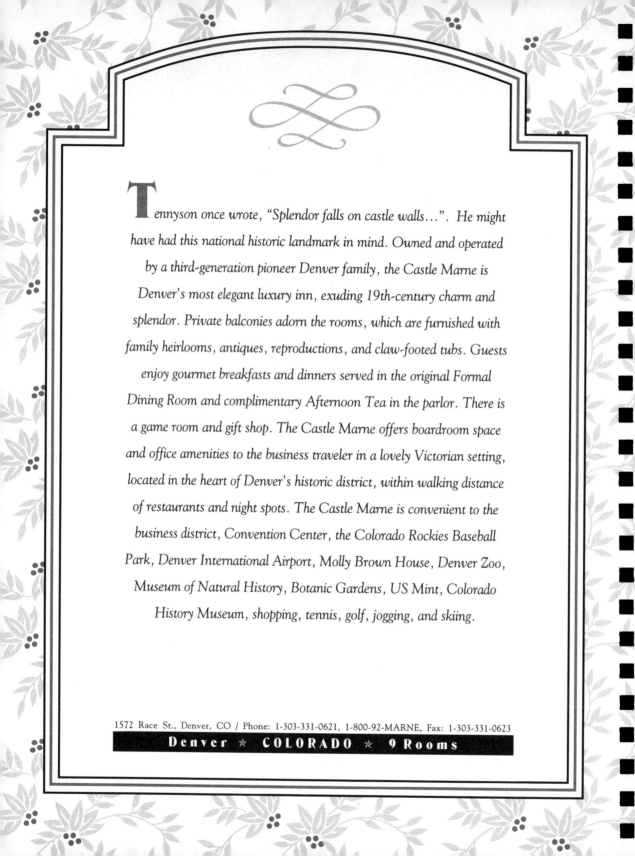

Tennyson once wrote, "Splendor falls on castle walls...". He might have had this national historic landmark in mind. Owned and operated by a third-generation pioneer Denver family, the Castle Marne is Denver's most elegant luxury inn, exuding 19th-century charm and splendor. Private balconies adorn the rooms, which are furnished with family heirlooms, antiques, reproductions, and claw-footed tubs. Guests enjoy gourmet breakfasts and dinners served in the original Formal Dining Room and complimentary Afternoon Tea in the parlor. There is a game room and gift shop. The Castle Marne offers boardroom space and office amenities to the business traveler in a lovely Victorian setting, located in the heart of Denver's historic district, within walking distance of restaurants and night spots. The Castle Marne is convenient to the business district, Convention Center, the Colorado Rockies Baseball Park, Denver International Airport, Molly Brown House, Denver Zoo, Museum of Natural History, Botanic Gardens, US Mint, Colorado History Museum, shopping, tennis, golf, jogging, and skiing.

1572 Race St., Denver, CO / Phone: 1-303-331-0621, 1-800-92-MARNE, Fax: 1-303-331-0623

Denver ✶ COLORADO ✶ 9 Rooms

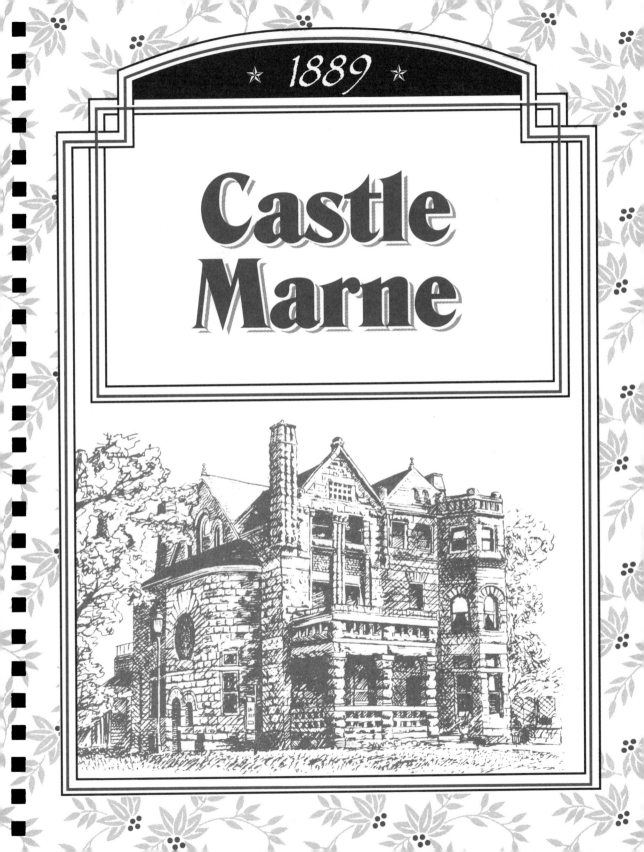

⋆ 1889 ⋆

Castle
Marne

Chicken Liver Pate

1 lb.	Chicken livers
1	Onion, medium, chopped
1/4 lb.	Butter
1/2 t.	Thyme
1	Bay leaf
12	Mushrooms, large, chopped
1/4 c.	Brandy, bourbon, rum or ...
1/2 t.	Salt
1/4 t.	Pepper

Rinse the chicken livers very well. If you do not rinse the livers well, the pâté will have a bitter taste. Split the livers and trim off any fat and connective tissue. Melt butter in a skillet or saucepan. Add livers and onions. Stir over medium heat for 10 minutes. Add thyme, bay leaf, and mushrooms. Stir frequently while cooking 5 minutes more. Discard bay leaf and pour mixture into blender. Add brandy, salt, and pepper. Blend 2 minutes. Pour into soufflé dish and garnish.

At the Castle Marne, we put our pâté into individual dishes of approximately 1/3-cup size and garnish with a sprig of fresh rosemary and serve this with homemade crackers or Pepperidge Farm "butterfly" crackers, and sliced boiled eggs, and capers or cornichons.

Makes One Pint

Mango Shrimp Wontons

48	Shrimp, small, peeled, deveined
MARINADE:	
1 c.	Sherry
1 c.	Soy sauce
4 T.	Flour
4 T.	Cold water
1 pkg.	Wonton skins
1	Mango, ripe, peeled and diced
8	Scallions, thinly sliced
4 c.	Vegetable oil
1 Jar	Hoisin sauce

Combine sherry and soy sauce. Add peeled shrimp; marinate for 20 minutes. Drain well. Combine water and flour into a paste. Set aside.

Lay out wonton skins and brush two edges with the flour/water mixture. In the center of each wonton, place one shrimp and a couple of pieces of mango and scallions. Carefully fold over two edges of wonton to meet the brushed edges, form a triangle, sealing tightly. Heat oil in large, deep-sided fry pan or electric fryer to 350 degrees. NOTE: Use extreme caution when frying with oil; maintain a constant temperature.

Fry wontons five or six at a time, turning occasionally so both sides cook. Fry to a golden brown, and set aside to drain while you fry the rest in small batches.

Serve warm with Hoisin dipping sauce.

Makes 48 wontons

Spinach and Red Leaf Lettuce Salad

Combine vinegar and jam in blender. Add oil slowly, blending well. Toss lettuce with dressing.

Put two of the whole red lettuce leaves on chilled salad plates. Arrange lettuce and spinach on plates. Top with onion slices and kiwi.

Makes Two Servings

1 T.	Raspberry vinegar
1 T.	Raspberry jam
2 T.	Salad oil
3 c.	Spinach, washed, stemmed and torn
1	Red leaf lettuce, small head (reserve four leaves)
1	Red onion, small, sliced paper thin
1	Kiwi, sliced

Seafood Spinach Crepes a la Marne

This makes a very dramatic presentation, but is really quite easy to make and serve.

Squeeze moisture from spinach. Melt butter and stir in flour, cook until bubbly. Slowly stir in milk, cook until thickened. Add spinach and spices, set aside.

Heat oil, and sauté onion and garlic. Add mushrooms, cook until tender. Drain off any excess moisture, stir in Creamed Spinach, seafood, lemon juice, tarragon, salt, and pepper. Preheat oven to 375 degrees.

Spoon about 1/3 c. of filling on each crepe. Roll to enclose filling. Place in lightly greased 12 x 9-inch baking dish. Sprinkle with cheese, bake in oven about 15 minutes or until filling is heated through.

Makes Four Servings

CREAMED SPINACH:

1 c.	Spinach, fresh, chopped
2 T.	Butter or margarine
2 T.	Flour
1 c.	Milk
	Salt and pepper (to taste)

SEAFOOD FILLING:

1 t.	Vegetable oil
1/2	Onion, medium, chopped
1	Garlic clove, diced
1/2 c.	Mushrooms, sliced
8 oz.	Fresh crab, small cooked shrimp, bay scallops, or a combination
2 T.	Lemon juice, fresh
1/4 t.	Dried leaf tarragon
1/2 t.	Salt
1/4 t.	Pepper
8	6-1/2-inch Crepes
1 c.	Swiss cheese, shredded

Pumpkin Bisque

1 T. Butter
1 Onion, large, diced
1-1/2 lbs. Pumpkin, diced or 3 c. pumpkin puree, home made or canned
6 c. Chicken stock
3 T. All purpose flour
1/2 t. Salt
1/4 c. Parsley, chopped

Melt the butter in large saucepan. Add diced onions and sauté until golden. Add the pumpkin and chicken stock. Cook over medium heat 10 minutes. Take out 1 c. of pumpkin/chicken mixture and add flour. Stir with whisk until all lumps are gone. Add the flour mixture to the soup and stir with whisk. Cook 5 minutes, whisking occasionally to cook the flour. Adjust seasonings and add parsley. Serve with croutons.

Makes Eight Servings

Pumpkins and Squash

These are new world plants and had been cultivated for an extensive period prior to European arrival. Native Americans have grown both winter and summer squash, pumpkins, and watermelons for hundreds of years. Pumpkins, for example, are used in cookies, muffins, breads, and soups. The Pueblo Indian tribes use squash and their blossoms in their contributions to the Rocky Mountain Cuisine.

Oven-Poached Rainbow Trout with Cucumber Dill Sauce

4 Rainbow Trout, 12-14 oz., very fresh
1/2 c. White wine
1 c. Water
2 Lemons, juice only
Paprika
1/2 c. Sour cream
1/4 c. Plain yogurt
1 t. Tamari Soy Sauce
1/4 c. Cucumber, finely grated
1 T. Dill, fresh, minced

Blend together sour cream, yogurt, soy sauce, and grated cucumber. Chill well, up to 3 hours, so flavors blend.

Preheat oven to 325 degrees. Wash, pat dry and de-bone trout. Place in buttered dish and pour water and wine over fish. Sprinkle lemon juice and paprika over all. Bake in oven for 35 to 40 minutes or until fish is firm and flakes easily with fork. Serve sauce over fish garnished with fresh dill.

Makes Four Servings

Welsh Rarebit

"This is another entrée served to our guests at a formal Victorian Luncheon. Legend has it that only the wealthy land owners in Wales could afford game for dinner. The lower classes had to make do with a dish of melted cheese served over toast or biscuits. It was jokingly referred to as a 'rare' or tasty 'bit' of rabbit" (Diane Peiker, The Castle Marne).

Melt butter in a double boiler, stir in beer. When heated, stir in grated cheese (use fork). When cheese is melted, stir in eggs, salt, pepper, and lemon juice.

Serve immediately over biscuits or toast points.

Makes Twelve Servings

2 T.	Butter
16 oz.	Dark beer
2 lbs.	Cheddar cheese, grated
2	Eggs, slightly beaten
2 T.	Worcestershire sauce
1/2 t.	Salt
1/8 t.	Red pepper (Cayenne)
2 t.	Lemon juice, fresh
	Toasted biscuit or toast points

"Denver Dry Goods Tea Room" Chicken a la King

For decades, Denverites enjoyed dining at the venerable old "Denver Dry Goods Tea Room". After they closed, this recipe became available. At the Marne, we enjoy serving this local favorite at our Victorian Luncheons.

Melt butter in large saucepan. Whisk in flour, cooking over moderate heat a few minutes. Gradually add chicken broth, whisking and cooking until thickened. Whisk in Half & Half. Simmer over low heat about 20 minutes. Add more chicken broth for desired consistency. Add chicken, bell peppers, mushrooms, salt, and pepper. Cook over low heat until heated through.

Serve in pastry shells or phyllo cups.

Makes Eight Servings

2	Butter or margarine (sticks)
1-1/2 c.	Flour
~ 8 c.	Chicken broth
1 c.	Half & Half
1 lb.	Chicken breasts, cooked, skinned, diced
1	Red pepper, large, cut into 1/4-inch strips
1/2 lb.	Mushrooms, sliced, sautéed in butter
	Salt, white pepper (to taste)
	Baked puff pastry shells or phyllo dough cups

The King's Rum Cakes

This is fast becoming one of the favorite Tea Time treats at the Castle.

2/3 c.	Butter (softened) or margarine
1-3/4 c.	Sugar
2	Eggs
2 t.	Vanilla
3 c.	Cake flour, sifted
2-1/2 t.	Baking powder
1 t.	Salt
1-1/4 c.	Milk

Set oven at 350 degrees. Cream butter, adding sugar gradually. Add eggs and vanilla. Beat until light and fluffy. Sift dry ingredients together, add to creamed mixture slowly, alternately adding milk. Beat 1 minute. Bake in greased, bundt-style muffin cups for approximately 20 minutes. Cool slightly.

RUM SAUCE:

1/4 lb.	Butter
1 c.	Sugar
1/4 c.	Water
1/2 c.	Rum

Melt butter. Add sugar and water. Stir constantly over high heat about 5 minutes. Be sure sugar is dissolved. Remove from heat. Add rum.

Soak warm cakes in rum sauce. Continually spoon rum sauce over tops of cakes (about one hour).

CRÈME ANGLAISE:

2 c.	Half & Half
3	Egg yolks
1/4 c.	Sugar, granulated
2 T.	Frangelico liquer
1/4 t.	Vanilla extract

In medium-size saucepan, heat Half & Half until just before boiling. In medium-size bowl, beat egg yolks and sugar at high speed until it becomes pale yellow and begins to thicken. At low speed, add hot Half & Half in a slow stream. Return mixture to saucepan and cook over low heat, stirring constantly until crème begins to thicken and coats spoon.

Remove from heat and stir in liqueur and vanilla. Keep warm until ready to serve. Makes 2 cups.

Raspberries, fresh

TO SERVE: Put a large spoonful of Anglaise sauce on dessert plate. Place cake in middle and drizzle Anglaise sauce over cake. Sprinkle with a few fresh raspberries.

Makes Eighteen Small Cakes

The Queen's Royal Scones

We have tasted scones from many tea rooms, and truly believe that this is the finest recipe we have tested.

In a large bowl, stir together the flour, sugar, baking powder, and soda until thoroughly blended. A pastry cutter or wire whisk works well. Using a pastry cutter, cut the butter into the flour mixture until it resembles cornmeal. Stir in the currants. Make a well in the center of the flour mixture and add the buttermilk all at once. Stir with a fork until the batter pulls away from the side of the bowl.

3-1/4 c.	All-purpose flour
3/4 c.	Sugar
2-1/2 t.	Baking powder
1/2 t.	Baking soda
3/4 c.	Butter, unsalted, firm, cut into small pieces
3/4 c.	Currants, dried, softened
1 c.	Buttermilk

Gather the dough together with your hands into a ball. On a lightly floured board, roll or pat the ball of dough into a circle. Using a smaller heart- or daisy-shaped cookie cutter, cut into individual scones. Place 1-1/2 inches apart on lightly greased baking sheets. If you wish, brush the tops of the scones with buttermilk, and sprinkle with sugar.

Bake in 425 degree oven for 12 minutes or until the tops are light brown. Serve warm with crème fraiche and raspberry jam or honey butter.

Makes Twenty-Four Scones

Melissa's Shortbread

We are certain you will agree with our guests, "these are to die for."

1/2 c.	Butter, soft
1/2 c.	Sugar
1/2 t.	Vanilla extract
1/4 t.	Almond extract
1 c.	All purpose flour
2 T.	Cornstarch
1/8 t.	Salt

Preheat oven to 325 degrees. Cream the butter, then add sugar and cream together until fluffy. Beat in vanilla and almond extracts. Sift flour, corn starch and salt. Work the dry ingredients into the creamed mixture with a pastry cutter. The mixture will be crumbly. Gather the dough lightly into a ball. Place the dough in an ungreased 10-inch pie pan or loose-bottomed tart pan. Using the fingers, press dough into a layer of uniform thickness. Be sure the dough is well pressed down. Use a thin knife to draw the dough slightly away from the edges. Make a decoration on the dough by pressing the tines of a fork into it. Mark with a knife into 16-18 wedges.

Bake in the center of preheated oven, until it is pale gold and feels firm when touched lightly, about 40 minutes. DO NOT let it turn brown, because the flavor will not be what it should be. Gently re-score the slices with a sharp knife after it has been out of the oven for approximately 10 minutes. If you wish, sprinkle with coarsely-ground, colored sugar before baking.

Serve warm.

Makes Eight Servings

Four O'Clock Tea Cakes

"This recipe was served by Diane's mother for bridge parties and at Tea Time," Jim Peiker.

Break graham crackers into blender container, blend thoroughly. Add broken nuts, and process. Melt butter and chocolate in saucepan, add sugar and beaten eggs. Simmer about a minute, stirring constantly.

Add cracker/nut mixture. Blend thoroughly, cool. Pat firmly into greased bread loaf pan.

Cream together butter and cream cheese until fluffy. While beating, sift in powdered sugar, a little at a time, and beat until fluffy. Add vanilla, cream, and salt and blend well. (You may need to add extra sugar or cream to get the right consistency. In hot weather, the icing will not hold consistency for piping.)

Frost with butter icing and decorettes (candy silver balls).

Makes 24 Squares

20	Double graham crackers
1/2 c.	Walnuts, broken
1	Butter, stick
1 sq.	Chocolate
3/4 c.	Sugar
2	Eggs, beaten

BUTTER ICING

6 T.	Butter, softened
1	Cream cheese, 8-oz. pkg, softened
1	Powdered sugar, 16-oz. pkg.
1 t.	Vanilla extract, pure Salt (to taste)
1-4 T.	Heavy cream

French Toast with Creamy Peach-Pecan Filling

Good anytime of the year, but especially delicious in the fall when Colorado's famous Western Slope Elberta Peaches are available.

Beat cream cheese until light and fluffy. Add peaches, pecans, and honey, blend. Cut almost through bread slices (leave a bit of a "hinge").

Heat griddle or large skillet to 350 degrees. Mix eggs, Half & Half, vanilla (or liqueur), and pour into shallow dish or pie pan.

Place about a tablespoon or so of mixture in the pocket of the bread. Carefully dip bread in egg mixture, turning to coat both sides. Fry in skillet about 2 to 3 minutes on each side, or until golden brown.

Serve with warmed maple syrup.

Makes Six Servings

1 pkg.	Cream cheese, 8 oz., softened
1 c.	Peaches, fresh, chopped
1/2 c.	Pecans, chopped
1	Baguette of French bread, cut diagonally about 1" thick
6	Eggs (lightly beaten)
1-1/2 c.	Half & Half
1 t.	Vanilla (substitute 1/4 c. orange liqueur, optional)

Leadville's gold and silver days brought desperados such as Billy the Kid, Doc Holiday, and Butch Cassidy to the Delaware Hotel. Today, over 100 years later, the Delaware remains Leadville's "Crown Jewel." Carefully renovated, the Victorian architecture reflects a gentle charm with its oak paneling, crystal chandeliers, and period antiques. Thirty-six guestrooms and suites are appointed with brass and iron bed frames, heirloom-style quilts, and lace curtains, each with a private bath and cable TV. Callaway's restaurant serves Rocky Mountain cuisine and favorite local dishes. In-house conference facilities accommodate groups up to 40 and banquets to 100. The surrounding national forests, lakes, and tallest mountain peaks in Colorado create an extraordinary outdoor recreational area with golf, hiking, white water rafting, fishing, hunting, bicycling, snowmobiling, and nordic and alpine skiing (within minutes), to name just a few. The town of Leadville boasts the National Mining Hall of Fame, museums, Tabor Opera House, railroad, four-wheel tours, and numerous distinctive shops.

700 Harrison Avenue, Leadville, CO / Phone: 1-719-486-1418, 1-800-748-2004, Fax: 1-719-486-2214

Leadville ✷ COLORADO ✷ 36 Rooms

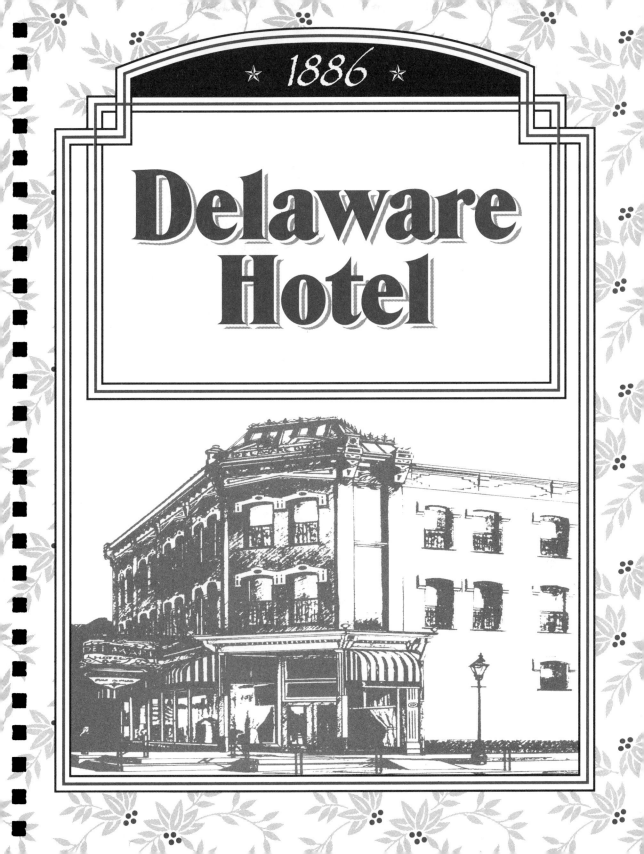

Callaway's Crab Melt

1	Croissant, 3 oz.
4 to 6 oz.	Crabmeat
4 oz.	Monterey Jack cheese (2 slices)
	Lemon Dill Hollandaise Sauce (see recipe below)
Pinch	Paprika

Slice croissant in half lengthwise, butter and grill for 1 to 2 minutes until very light brown. Warm crab by placing in saucepan in a 400-degree oven for 3 to 4 minutes. Take crab out and place inside croissant, top with jack cheese and again put in 400-degree oven for approximately 2 minutes. Take out and top with Lemon Dill Hollandaise, sprinkle with paprika. Enjoy!

LEMON DILL HOLLANDAISE SAUCE (MAKE FIRST):

3	Egg yolks, separated, room temperature
1 lb.	Sweet cream butter, melted, clarified
1	Lemon
1 t.	Worcestershire sauce
1/2 t.	White pepper
1 t.	Dill weed (1/2 bunch if fresh)

Place 3 egg yolks, juice of 1 lemon, worcestershire sauce, and white pepper in double boiler. Whip and cook until mixture starts to thicken. Remove from heat immediately. Take warm (110 degrees) clarified butter and incorporate into egg mixture until it resembles sauce, stir dill weed into mixture. Serve.

Makes One Serving

Chix Dijon alias "Tabor Chicken"

1	Chicken breast, 6 oz. (pounded)
	Flour
2 T.	Olive oil
1 oz.	White wine
1 oz.	Chicken broth
Pinch + half	Garlic, minced
Pinch	Shallots, finely chopped
1/2 t.	Horseradish
1 t.	Dijon mustard
1/4 c.	Heavy whipping cream
1 T.	Parsley, fresh, chopped

Heat olive oil in a 6-inch skillet, flour dredge the chicken, and put in skillet on low heat. Cook chicken halfway, add wine. Reduce. Add chicken stock, garlic, and shallots. Reduce. Add horseradish, Dijon mustard, and whipping cream. Reduce. Add parsley. Eat and enjoy!

Makes One Serving

Trout Almondine

Trim the fillets by removing fat and fins on each side, trim the head off at neck, and remove pin bones at top of body with needle nose pliers. Heat butter over medium heat. Dredge trout in flour mixture. Sauté trout 4 to 5 minutes until browned. Turn once and cook 1 minute.

At the same time, start sauce by combining liqueur, garlic, shallots, lemon juice, and heavy cream. Reduce in half, then add almonds. Spread sauce over fillet and garnish with parsley and lemon zest.

Makes Six Servings

6	*Trout, 8 oz. fillets*
3 T.	*Clarified butter*
	Flour, salt, pepper

SAUCE:

2 T.	*Frangelico liqueur*
1 T.	*Garlic*
1 T.	*Shallots*
1 t.	*Lemon juice*
1-1/2 c.	*Heavy cream*
3 T.	*Almonds, toasted*

Garnish (parsley and lemon zest)

Native Fish

The two most beloved native fish of the Rockies are trout and Walleye Pike. The cold water streams and lakes provide habitat for numerous types of trout, which provided early European settlers with a welcome change in their diet. The native trout population has long been supplemented by trout farms that provide the chefs of the Rockies with a ready year-round supply with which their talent can be applied to this Rocky Mountain delicacy.

The Walleye Pike is sweet tasting and enjoys enormous popularity in the Northern Rockies. The chefs often compliment pike's flavor with a delicate sauce. Walleye pike is a treat not to be missed!

Vegetarian Green Chili with Blue Corn Chips

12	Anaheim chiles, roasted and peeled
2 c.	Tomatillas, diced
2 c.	Tomatoes, diced
1/2 c.	Green peppers, diced
1/2 c.	Red peppers, diced
1/2 c.	Yellow onion, diced
3	Jalapeño peppers, diced
3 T.	Olive oil
3	Garlic cloves, minced
1/2 c.	Black beans, cooked
1 t.	Black pepper, fresh ground
1/2 T.	White pepper
1 T.	Mexican oregano
2 T.	Cumin
1 c.	Tomatoes, diced
1/2	Cilantro, bunch
4 c.	Water
1/4 c.	Roux

Sauté fresh vegetables over medium heat until soft. Add the spices, 1 c. of tomatoes, and water. Cover and simmer for 2 hours, stirring occasionally. Coarsely chop the cilantro and add to the mixture. Add the roux to mixture, stirring continuously until thickened.

Serve with blue corn chips (see recipe below).

BLUE CORN CHIPS:

12	Blue Corn Tortillas
	Vegetable oil

Cut tortillas in sixths. Fry in oil over medium high heat, approximately one minute per side.

Makes Eight Servings

Elk Chops with Wild Mushroom-Marsala Sauce

6	Elk chops, 6 oz.
1 oz.	Dry wild mushrooms (oyster, morel, woodear)
1 T.	Shallots
1 T.	Garlic
1 t.	Pepper, fresh ground
1/4 c.	Marsala wine
4 T.	Olive oil
2-1/2 c.	Demi-glaze
	Flour
	Parsley sprigs, fresh

Soak mushrooms till pliable. Dredge chops in flour. Sauté chops in olive oil on medium heat, 2 minutes per side. Transfer to ovenproof dish and bake in 400-degree oven until medium. Toss shallots and garlic in sauté pan until soft. Deglaze the pan with the Marsala wine. When reduced to half, add demi-glaze and mushrooms. Reduce heat and simmer until thick. Pour over chops and sprinkle with fresh parsley sprigs.

Makes Six Servings

Roasted Buffalo Au Jus

Place carrots, onions, celery, and water in bottom of roasting pan. Prepare the roast by cutting small incisions in outer layer and inserting the garlic and peppercorns in the incisions. Spread the Dijon mustard over the entire roast. Then sprinkle with rosemary, thyme leaves, and salt. Cover and roast in 300-degree oven until temperature on the meat thermometer at the center of the roast is 135 to 140 degrees. Remove roast from pan. Place roasting pan on medium heat. Deglaze pan with port wine. Add 5 cups of water and reduce to half. Strain vegetables.

Serve Au Jus on side.

Makes Ten Servings

2	Carrots, roughly chopped
1	Yellow onion, chopped
2	Celery stalks, chopped
1/2 c.	Water
1	Buffalo roast (8-12 lb.)
6	Garlic cloves
2 T.	Black peppercorns, cracked
2 T.	Dijon mustard
1 T.	Rosemary leaves
1 T.	Thyme leaves
2 T.	Salt
1/4 c.	Port wine
5 c.	Water

Southwestern Rice

Sauté rice over medium heat for 4 to 5 minutes. Add vegetables, garlic, and spices. Continue to cook until onions are clear and rice has browned. Add water and nuts, cover, and let come to a boil. Turn off, leave in a warm area undisturbed for 1 hr. and 15 minutes, then serve.

Makes Eight Servings

2 c.	White rice
3 T.	Olive oil
1	Tomato, chopped
1/2 c.	Green pepper, chopped
1/2 c.	Red pepper, chopped
1/2 c.	Yellow pepper, chopped
1	Anaheim chile, chopped
3	Garlic cloves, chopped
1 T.	Oregano
2 T.	Cumin
1 T.	Chili powder
2 T.	Parsley, fresh, chopped
4 c.	Water
1/2 c.	Piñon nuts, toasted

3 Ducks
2 Carrots, *chopped*
2 Celery stalks, *chopped*
1 Yellow onion, *chopped*
  Necks and innards
  Water
2 T. Pepper, *fresh ground*
2 T. Rosemary leaves
1 T. Salt
1 T. Garlic, *granulated*
1 T. Thyme
2 c. Water

Place the roughly cut vegetables, necks, innards, and water in the bottom of a roasting pan. Trim excess fat off ducks and discard. Cut wing so only first joint is left. Pepper the ducks, place in roasting pan, and sprinkle with herbs and spices. Roast covered at 300 degrees until the internal temperature of the duck is 110. Uncover, increasing the heat to 375 degrees. Cook until lightly browned on top. Rotate bird so back is up. Cook until bird reaches 145 degrees. Remove from pan and cool in refrigerator. When cool, debone and slice the duck.

Deglaze roasting pan with 2 cups of water. Reduce by one-fourth. Strain vegetables. Place stock in refrigerator overnight to skim off fat.

To DEBONE BIRD: a) Split breast down center; b) cut out backbone on each side leaving equal halves; c) remove rib cage by slicing thumb down between bone and meat. d) Make two slits at leg bone and wing joint. Twist bone and hold meat leaving meat on the cavity; e) twist out thigh bone down underneath holding meat securely.

CHAMBORD SAUCE:
1 lb. Raspberries, *frozen, thawed*
      Duck stock
1/2 c. Water
2 T. Lemon juice, *fresh*
2 T. Orange juice concentrate
1 T. Lime juice, *fresh*
Zest Lemon, lime, and orange
1/4 c. Honey
2 T. Cornstarch
2 oz. Chambord liqueur
1 t. Shallots

      Raspberries, *fresh*

Simmer raspberries in duck stock, water, and juices for 1 hour. Strain raspberry mixture to remove seeds. Return to heat, adding zests and honey. Simmer for 5 minutes. Thicken with cornstarch. Stir in Chambord liqueur.

To SERVE: Spoon the Chambord Sauce onto a plate. Fan the duck meat, and spoon more of the sauce over the duck. Garnish with fresh raspberries.

Makes Six Servings

Game Birds

Native and introduced game birds in the Rocky Mountains are numerous. Waterfowl include ducks and geese, and upland game birds range from the various grouse, to quail, doves, chukar, pheasants, and wild turkeys. The wild turkey was at one time domesticated by the Anasazi, who also used the feathers to weave into a net of yucca fiber to make an early down quilt. Seems like it would be a bit ticklish!

These birds were a featured entrée in mid- to late-1800s menus throughout the Rockies. They were prepared by stewing, roasting, and spit roasting. Today, hunting for game birds is a favorite fall pastime; however, the non-hunter can usually order most of these birds, or their domesticated equivalents, from their butcher shop.

High in the San Luis Valley, this secluded retreat is situated at the heart of Colorado's legendary 100,000-acre Zapata Ranch. Once a turn-of-the-century livestock operation, it is now home to one of the largest bison herds in the country. Original ranch buildings which house guests are constructed with rough-hewn logs, while the bathrooms' claw-foot tubs and pedestal sinks blend charm with convenience. Antiques indigenous to the San Luis Valley accent rooms and public areas. The Inn's caretaker built the beautiful handmade beds, and the caretaker's cottage was once the old stagecoach stop. The Great Sand Dunes Country Inn's restaurant is widely recognized for its excellent regional cuisine: a sophisticated combination of fresh, local produce and products prepared with marvelous flare. Other amenities appreciated by guests are the Inn's 18-hole golf course, sauna, hot tub, heated pool, and health club. Guests can also enjoy the tour of the bison ranch to see the herd numbering near 3,000. Significant area attractions include Great Sand Dunes National Monument, Alamosa Wildlife Refuge, and the historic Cumbres & Toltec Scenic Railroad.

5303 Hwy 150, Mosca, CO / Phone: 1-719-378-2356, 1-800-284-9213, Fax: 1-719-378-2428

Mosca ★ COLORADO ★ 15 Rooms

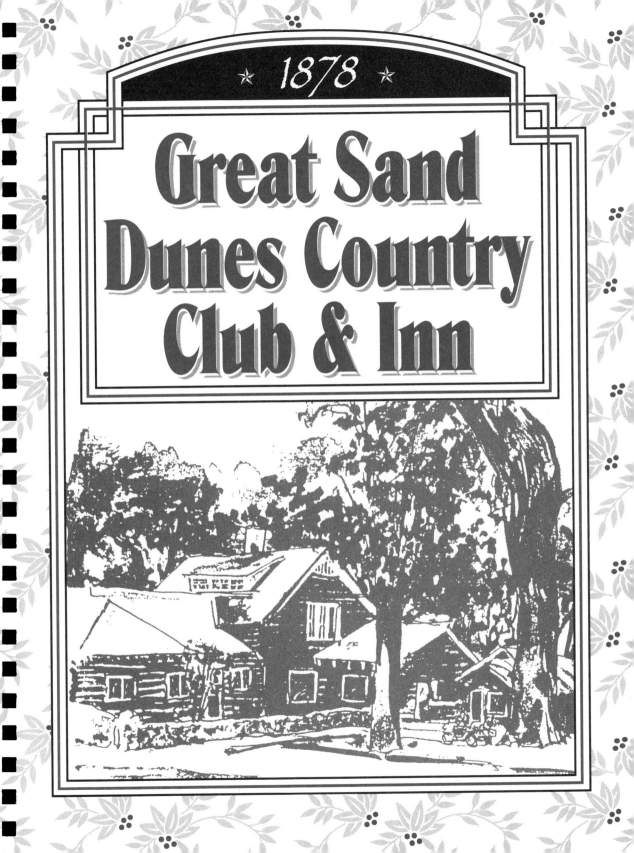

☆ 1878 ☆

Great Sand Dunes Country Club & Inn

Chilled Tomato Soup with Cilantro Cream

Pascal Sauton, a member of Chaine des Rotisseurs, is a native of Paris, France. He came to the Great Sand Dunes in 1994 via Paris, France; Cayenne, French Guyana; and Manhattan, New York. He has brought an extraordinary sophistricated culinary skill and precise cooking style to this remote high mountain get-away.

3 c.	Chicken stock
2 T.	Olive oil
1/2 c.	Onions, thickly sliced
1/2 c.	Leeks, white, thickly sliced
1/4 c.	Fennel, thickly sliced
1/3 c.	Celery, coarsely chopped
1	Sweet red pepper, large, split, seeded, thickly sliced
2	Garlic cloves, large, peeled, chopped
6	Tabasco, drops
1 T.	Tomato paste
1/2 t.	Salt
3 c.	Tomatoes, ripe, 1/2-inch dice
1/2 c.	Tomato juice
Pinch	Sugar

CILANTRO CREAM:

1/2 c.	Cilantro, picked from the stem and rinsed
4 T.	Sour cream
2	Limes, juice
	Salt and pepper (to taste)

Heat the chicken stock in a small saucepan. Heat the oil in a large pot. Add the onions, leeks, fennel, celery, red pepper, garlic, and Tabasco. Cook until the vegetables are very soft, about 10 minutes, stirring often. Reduce heat to medium, add the tomato paste, and stir for 3 minutes. Add the hot chicken stock, bring to a boil, add the salt, and simmer for 20 minutes.

Add fresh tomatoes, return to a boil, and simmer for 10 more minutes. Remove the soup from the heat and set aside to cool. Refrigerate for 2 hours. Blend the soup in a blender until smooth. Add the tomato juice, sugar, and taste for seasoning. Strain and chill until ready to serve.

Chop the cilantro and add to the sour cream with the lime juice. Add salt and pepper to taste.

TO SERVE: Pour the cold tomato soup into chilled soup bowls and place a spoon full of cilantro cream in the middle.

Makes Four Servings

Bison, Apple, and Black Bean Chili

Place the black beans in a medium saucepan and add 6 c. of water, bring to a boil over moderate high heat, and boil for 3 minutes. Remove from the heat and let stand for 1 hour.

Meanwhile, roast the poblanos, bell peppers, and habanero under the broiler as close to the heat as possible or over a gas flame, turning frequently until blackened all over. Transfer to a paper bag and let steam for 10 minutes. Peel the chiles and pepper under running water and remove the core, seeds, and ribs. Drain and pat dry. Place them in a food processor with the tomatillos and scallions, and purée until smooth.

Drain the black beans and return them to the saucepan. Add the bacon, bay leaves, and 6 more cups of water. Bring to a boil over high heat. Cover, simmer over low heat, until beans are tender. Drain, reserving 1 c. of liquid. Discard the bay leaves, and cut the bacon in 1/2-inch pieces and set aside.

Heat 2 T. of oil in a large cast-iron casserole. Season the bison cubes with salt and pepper. Add some of the meat to the casserole in a single layer and cook over high heat, until well browned all over, about 5 minutes. Transfer to a plate and brown remaining in batches.

Heat 1 T. of oil in the casserole. Add the onion and garlic, and sauté until translucent. Return the browned bison meat to the casserole with the chile purée, sugar, cumin, and 1 t. of salt. Bring to boil, then lower heat, simmer until meat is very tender, about 2 hours. Stir in black beans, cubed bacon, and apples with the reserve cooking liquid.

Season the chili with salt and pepper, and spoon into bowls. Serve with cornbread and sour cream.

Makes Six to Eight Servings

1-1/2 c.	Black beans, dried
4	Poblano chiles, medium
4	Green bell peppers, medium
1	Habanero chile, medium
10	Tomatillos, medium, husked, rinsed and quartered
5	Scallions, coarsely chopped
1 lb.	Bacon, smoked
2	Bay leaves
4	Apples, peeled, seeded, diced
3 T.	Vegetable oil
2 lb.	Bison stewing meat, 1-inch cubes
	Salt, pepper, fresh ground
1	Onion, medium, finely chopped
6	Garlic cloves, minced
1 T.	Sugar
1 T.	Cumin, ground
1 t.	Salt
	Cornbread
	Sour cream

San Luis Valley Striped Bass with Honey-Ginger Vinaigrette

VINAIGRETTE:
- 2 T.   Rice vinegar
- 1 t.   Ginger, fresh grated
- 2 T.   Honey
- 1/2 c.   Sesame oil, pure
- 1 T.   Water, boiling

- 2 T.   Sesame oil, pure
- 2   Striped bass, fresh water, filets, 4 to 5 oz. each
- 10   Snow pea pods, stemmed, cut into thin strips
- 1 c.   Basmati rice, cooked

Combine the rice vinegar, ginger, and honey in a blender. Process for 30 seconds on high, and while motor running, slowly add the sesame oil and boiling water and process for 10 more seconds. Set aside.

In a heavy skillet, heat 2 T. sesame oil over medium-high heat. Sear the filets on both sides, skin side first, for 6 to 7 minutes per side. Set aside.

In the same pan, sauté the snow peas over low heat for 2 minutes or until tender.

To serve, place the warm rice on the center of 2 warm plates and place the fish on top of the rice, skin side up. Add the snow peas on top of the fish and sprinkle the vinaigrette over it.

Makes Two Servings

Goat Cheese Bricks with Endive Salad

- 1 c.   Goat cheese, white, soft, fresh
- 1-1/2 t.   Rosemary, fresh chopped
- 1-1/2 t.   Thyme, fresh chopped
- 3   Phyllo dough sheets
- 2 T.   Extra virgin olive oil
  Endive Salad (see recipe - next page)

Heat oven to 450 degrees. Mix the cheese and herbs and roll the mixture into four 2-inch balls. Cover and refigerate until ready to use.

Layer three phyllo sheets and cut into four 4 x 16-inch strips. Arrange into four stacks. Brush the top strips lightly with olive oil. Place a ball of cheese on the end of each stack of phyllo strips. Fold phyllo up over the cheese to form a triangle and roll until in tightly rolled triangles. Brush tops with olive oil. Place on a non-stick baking sheet and bake until golden brown, about 10 minutes. Serve with endive salad.

Makes Four Servings

Endive Salad

Separate the endive leaves and slice into long, thin strips. Combine remaining ingredients in a bowl and mix well. Pour over the endive leaves and toss.

Makes Four Servings

3	Endive, heads
1/2 t.	Lemon juice, fresh
2 T.	Peanut oil
2 t.	Sherry vinegar
2 t.	Peanuts, raw, cracked
1 t.	Chives, chopped
	Salt, pepper, fresh ground (to taste)

Lamb in Potato Crust with Mushroom Syrup

In a pan large enough to hold the mushrooms in a single layer, heat the butter until sizzling. Add the mushrooms with a pinch of salt and pepper and cook, stirring constantly, until the mushrooms are deep brown and have caramelized, about 15 to 20 minutes.

Add the shallots, garlic, and just enough water to cover mushrooms. Add the parsley and stir well, scraping any brown bits clinging to the pan. Transfer the mushrooms and broth to a smaller pot, and boil for 15 minutes. Strain broth through a fine mesh strainer and reduce over high heat, until there is 1/4 cup, set aside.

Heat 2 T. olive oil over medium high heat, until very hot. Sear the medallions of lamb about 10 seconds per side. Remove immediately from the pan. Season with salt and pepper, and set aside. Peel and shred potatoes (do not put in water). Lightly season with salt. Pat the shredded potatoes around each lamb medallion by pressing firmly between your hands so potatoes adhere.

In a large non-stick pan, heat 1/2 c. olive oil over medium heat. Add the lamb and cook until potatoes are brown and crisp on both sides. In a small saucepan, warm the mushroom syrup and whisk in 2 T. olive oil. Add the tomato, basil, salt, and pepper. Place one medallion on each of four warmed plates. Pour the sauce around each and garnish with a sprig of fresh basil.

Makes Four Servings

MUSHROOM SYRUP:

2 T.	Sweet butter
1 lb.	Mushrooms, white button, quartered
	Salt and pepper (to taste)
2	Shallots, peeled and sliced
1	Garlic clove, peeled, halved
2 c.	Water
2 T.	Parsley, minced

3/4 c.	Olive oil
2	Lamb racks, eyes trimmed, cut into eight 4-oz. medallions
	Salt and pepper (to taste)
4	Potatoes, medium
1/4 c.	Mushroom syrup
1	Tomato, medium, peeled, seeded, and diced
4	Basil leaves, cut into ribbons
4	Basil leaves, sprigs

Creme Brulee

(Should be prepared the day before)

1/2 c.	Heavy cream
1/2 c.	Milk
3	Egg yolks
1/3 c.+2 T.	Sugar
1	Vanilla bean, split in half lengthwise

Preheat oven to 375 degrees. In a small heavy pot, bring the cream, milk, and vanilla bean to a boil. In a small mixing bowl, cream egg yolks and sugar with a whisk, until fluffy. Pour the boiling cream and milk mixture over the egg yolk mixture, whipping constantly. Remove the vanilla bean and let cool.

Fill two ramekins with the mixture and place them in an ovenproof deep dish, with water coming half way up the ramekins. Cook in the oven for 45 minutes.

When cooked, allow to cool for 1 hour, then keep in refrigerator overnight. When ready to serve, spread evenly 1 T. of sugar on top of each custard. Place under the broiler until the sugar starts caramelizing and serve immediately.

Makes Two Servings

Black Bean Soup

Magdi Nafeh was the Great Sand Dunes' original chef. He opened the restaurant in 1990 and stayed for three seasons. A native of Cairo, Egypt, Magdi used a profusion of Mediterranean flavors and developed quite a following among Inn guests.

1 lb.	Black beans, rinsed and drained
1	Onion, medium, cut into quarters
4	Garlic cloves
4	Bay leaves
1 T.	Coriander, dry ground
1/2 T.	Cumin, dry ground
1 t.	Black pepper, ground
2 T.	Garlic, minced
1/4 c.	Olive oil
1 gal.	Chicken stock
1 T.	Salt

In a 2-gallon pot, combine the black beans, onion, bay leaves, coriander, cumin, and black pepper with 1-1/2 gallons of cold water. Bring to a boil, and simmer until the beans are tender (approximately 45 minutes at sea level, 60 minutes at 6,000 feet). Let beans cool after draining the water.

Sauté minced garlic in the olive oil. Purée the beans and cook briefly with some of the chicken stock, then add all of the stock and salt. Cook covered for 20 minutes.

Serve with strips of fried corn tortillas and diced green and red bell peppers.

Makes Ten Servings

Pasta with Shrimp and Jalapeno-Orange Sauce

Melt butter in heavy large skillet over medium-high heat. Add shrimp and cook until just pink, about 1 minute per side. Transfer shrimp to plate. Add shallots and jalapeño to skillet, sauté 1 minute. Add wine and bring to boil. Mix in orange juice and cream.

Boil until reduced to thin sauce, stirring occasionally, about 10 minutes. Season to taste with salt and pepper.

Cook pasta al dente. Drain. Bring sauce to simmer. Add shrimp and cook until heated through. Add pasta and toss well. Divide pasta among plates.

TO SERVE: Garnish with fresh parsley and serve.

Makes Four Servings

6 T.	Butter, unsalted
24	Shrimp, large, peeled, deveined
2 T.	Shallots, minced
1	Jalapeño chili, small, seeded, thinly sliced
1/2 c.	Dry white wine
1-1/2 c.	Orange juice
3/4 c.	Whipping cream
	Salt, pepper (to taste)
12 oz.	Angel hair pasta
	Parsley, fresh, minced

Fettuccini Natasha with Smoked Salmon

Cook noodles in salted boiling water until tender (approximately 4 minutes). Drain and refresh with ice water to prevent overcooking. Toss drained noodles with 1/2 T. olive oil.

In a 9-inch pan, cook shallots briefly in 1 T. butter on high heat. Add vodka and cook until almost dry. Add whipping cream, ocean salt, and white pepper and cook, stirring occasionally until sauce covers the back of a wooden spoon. Add smoked salmon. Toss pasta and salmon in sauce.

TO SERVE: Distribute among four bowls and sprinkle with fresh chopped basil.

Makes Four Servings

1 lb.	Smoked salmon, chopped
1 lb.	Fettuccini egg noodles
1/2 T.	Olive oil
2 T.	Shallots, minced
1 T.	Butter
3 oz.	Vodka
1 pt.	Whipping cream
2 t.	Ocean salt
1 t.	White pepper
	Basil, fresh, chopped

Potato Leek Soup with Fresh Thyme

Charlotte Dudek, a former chef to Denmark's Ambassador to the United Nations, brought her delicate Scandinavian touch to the 1993 season. She used fresh San Luis Valley ingredients and created a unique fare she called "Harvest Cooking."

1	Chicken, whole, 3 lb.
2	Yellow onions, chopped
2	Celery stalks, chopped
Scraps	Leeks
2	Garlic cloves
10	Peppercorns, white, whole
1	Thyme, bunch
1	Bay leaf
	Salt
6	Leeks, sliced, 1/4-inch rings
1	Yellow onion, large, diced
2	Garlic cloves, chopped
2 T.	Butter
1 pt.	Heavy cream
	Thyme, fresh
4	Potatoes, medium, cooked, chopped
	Salt and pepper (to taste)

Put chicken into 10-quart pot. Cover with cold water and bring to a boil. Skim all the fat. Add the onions, celery, leeks, garlic, peppercorns, thyme, bay leaf, and salt. Reduce heat and simmer for 2 hours. Add water, as necessary. Strain. Reserve chicken meat for sandwiches or salads.

Melt butter in heavy-bottom pot. Sauté leeks, onion, and garlic in butter for 5 minutes over medium heat. Add strained chicken stock and heavy cream. Cook for about 15 minutes. Add fresh chopped thyme, cooked potatoes, salt, and pepper (to taste).

Garnish with sour cream and serve with whole grain bread.

Makes Four to Six Servings

Bison Steak

4	Bison steaks, 8 to 10 oz. each 1-1/2-inch thick, brushed with oil

HERB BUTTER:

2 T.	Parsley, chopped
2 T.	Cilantro, chopped
	Salt, pepper (to taste)
1/2 lb.	Butter, soft

Grill steaks 2 to 3 minutes on each side for rare to medium. Add salt and pepper.

Mix parsley, cilantro, salt, pepper, and butter well. Roll herb butter up in paper and let cool. Slice.

TO SERVE: Place two slices of herb butter on top of grilled steak. Serve steamed spring vegetables and baked, creamed, or fried potatoes on the side.

Makes Four Servings

Buffalo, or More Properly, Bison

Meeting the herds of buffalo on the plains for the first time must have been one of those singular experiences of a lifetime for the people of the frontier. The first time I saw a huge herd of buffalo was at the Great Sand Dunes County Club and Inn. I at once experienced that eerie feeling of being transported back to an earlier time, and had a near-simultaneous feeling of awe, similar to my first experience up close and personal with a whale in the North Atlantic.

The massive herds long sustained Native Americans and early frontier people, but soon their very numbers devalued the individual bison, for providing a variety of "products" — hide, bone, and meat — until they were slaughtered only for their hides and their tongues. The herds were depleted nearly out of existence.

Today, you can enjoy the wonderful taste of American bison prepared by many of the fine featured chefs. If you want to see the second largest private herd in the country go to the high-country of southern Colorado. The increase in the herd size reflects the increase in popularity of buffalo. And no wonder. Today, people are seeking foods which are natural, low in cholesterol, low in saturated fats, low in calories, and high in nutrient value. The American Bison Association commissioned research, which resulted in the following very revealing comparison data:

Bison Nutritional Information *(research conducted by independent producer and laboratory - 1988)*			
3 oz serving	Calories	Fat	Cholesterol
Bison*	93	1.8 g	43 mg
Turkey	125	3.0 g	59 mg
Chicken	140	3.0 g	55 mg
Beef	183	8.7 g	55 mg
American Heart Assoc. Recommendations:	177	7.7 g	77 mg

Bison fed corn ration for 90 days prior to processing (unpublished data)

Trout with Quinoa

QUINOA-BASIC RECIPE:
1-3/4 c. Water
    1 c. Quinoa

Rinse quinoa thoroughly, either by using a strainer or by running fresh water over the quinoa in a pot. Drain excess water. Place quinoa and water in a 1-1/2 quart saucepan and bring to a boil. Reduce to a simmer, cover, and cook until all of the water is absorbed (about 15 minutes). You will know that the quinoa is done when all the grains have turned from white to transparent and the spiral-like germ has separated.

Makes Three Cups

3 c. Black quinoa, cooked (see recipe above)
4 c. Tomato juice
      Dill, chopped
      Salt, pepper (to taste)
  8   Trout filets
      White wine
2 T. Butter

Mix cooked quinoa and tomato juice. Heat over low flame until hot. Add chopped dill, salt, and pepper to taste. Bake trout in wine and butter, remove skin (about 5 minutes in the oven at 350 degrees).

TO SERVE: Place quinoa on plate, put baked trout on top, and decorate with dill.

Makes Four Servings

Roasted Lamb Chops with Onion-Apricot Compote

4 Lamb chops, French-cut per person

ONION-APRICOT COMPOTE:
8-oz. Butter (1 stick)
   6   Onions, red or white, diced
   2   Scallions, bunches, sliced
  20   Apricots, dried, chopped
6 T.   Honey
6 T.   Balsamic vinegar
       Parsley, bunch
       Salt and pepper (to taste)

Melt butter. Sauté onions and scallions until transparent. Add dried, chopped apricots, honey, and vinegar. Keep stirring until apricots are soft. Salt and pepper to taste. Add chopped parsley before serving.

TO SERVE: Place the roasted lamb chops on the onion-apricot compote. Serve with new roasted potatoes and vegetables of choice, such as grilled asparagus or sautéed spinach.

Makes Six Servings

Apple Crumbcake

Butter and flour a 7 x 9-inch baking pan. Sift flour, baking powder, cinnamon, and sugar into a large bowl. Add the butter, vanilla, lemon zest, and eggs. Mix well. Fold in apple slices and sour cream. Pour into the baking pan.

In a bowl, mix butter, flour, and sugar. Sprinkle over cake batter. Bake at 350 degrees for 30 minutes. Cool for about 15 minutes. Serve warm with cinnamon whipped cream.

Makes Four Servings

BATTER:

3/4 c.	Cake flour, sifted
1 T.	Baking powder
1 t.	Cinnamon
3/4 c.	Sugar
1/4 c.	Butter, unsalted, melted and cooled
2 T.	Vanilla extract
Zest	Lemon
2	Eggs
8	Apples, peeled, thinly sliced
1/2 c.	Sour cream

CRUMB TOPPING:

1/2 c.	Butter, unsalted, cut into small pieces
1-1/2 c.	Cake flour
3/4 c.	Light brown sugar
1 t.	Cinnamon
	Whipped cream

Cornbread

Preheat oven to 350 degrees. Butter and flour 7 x 9-inch baking pan. Sift flour, cornmeal, and baking powder into a large bowl. Whisk remaining ingredients together in a bowl, add to dry ingredients.

Mix well. Pour batter into baking pan. Bake for about 20 minutes until sides of pan come clean. Serve at room temperature.

Makes Four to Six Servings

1-1/2 c.	Cake flour, sifted
1/2 c.	Yellow cornmeal
1 T.	Baking powder
2/3 c.	Water
3	Eggs
1/2 c.	Butter, unsalted, melted
2 T.	Green chiles, chopped
3 T.	Brown sugar
1 t.	Salt
~ 1 c.	Fresh corn
2	Green onions, chopped

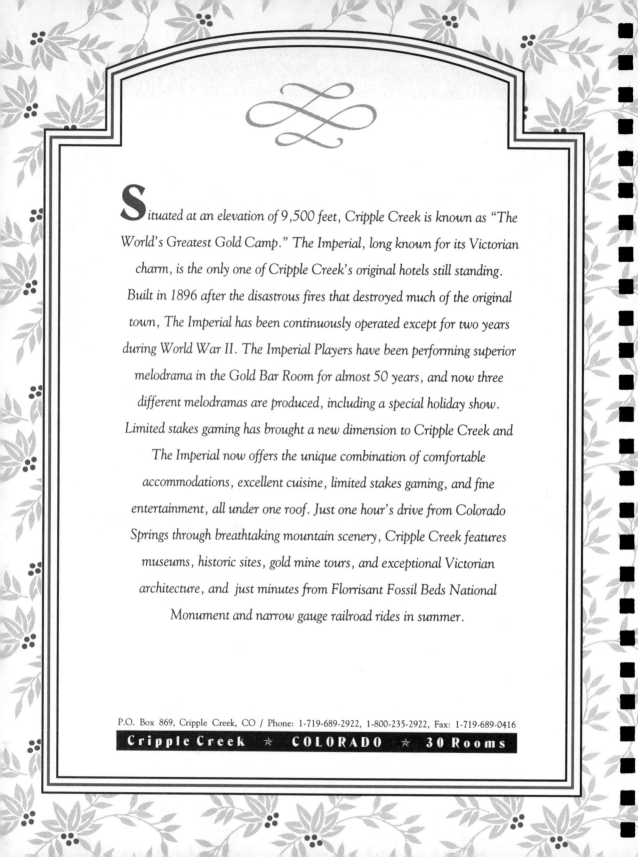

*S*ituated at an elevation of 9,500 feet, Cripple Creek is known as "The World's Greatest Gold Camp." The Imperial, long known for its Victorian charm, is the only one of Cripple Creek's original hotels still standing. Built in 1896 after the disastrous fires that destroyed much of the original town, The Imperial has been continuously operated except for two years during World War II. The Imperial Players have been performing superior melodrama in the Gold Bar Room for almost 50 years, and now three different melodramas are produced, including a special holiday show. Limited stakes gaming has brought a new dimension to Cripple Creek and The Imperial now offers the unique combination of comfortable accommodations, excellent cuisine, limited stakes gaming, and fine entertainment, all under one roof. Just one hour's drive from Colorado Springs through breathtaking mountain scenery, Cripple Creek features museums, historic sites, gold mine tours, and exceptional Victorian architecture, and just minutes from Florrisant Fossil Beds National Monument and narrow gauge railroad rides in summer.

P.O. Box 869, Cripple Creek, CO / Phone: 1-719-689-2922, 1-800-235-2922, Fax: 1-719-689-0416

Cripple Creek ★ COLORADO ★ 30 Rooms

* 1896 *

The Imperial Hotel

The "Imperial" Fruit Soup

1 c.   Prunes, pitted, diced
1 c.   Apricots, diced, dried
1 c.   Peaches, diced, dried
2 qts. Water, boiling
1/2   Lemon rind, grated
1/2 c. Sugar, granulated
2 T.   Cornstarch
Pinch   Salt

Cover the fruit with boiling water and let soak overnight, including the lemon rind. Next day, cook the fruit in the soaking water, until very soft. Mix the sugar and cornstarch together and add a small amount of the fruit mixture to make a paste. Add the paste to the fruit, then add the salt, and mix well.

Serve hot or cold.

Makes Eight Servings

Cheddar and Beer Soup

2-1/2 oz.   Butter
2 oz.   Onions
1-1/2 oz.   Celery
2-1/2 oz.   Flour
1-1/4 qt.   Chicken stock
4 oz.   Beer
1-1/2 lbs. Cheddar, grated
1 pt.   Half & Half
1 T.   Dijon mustard
1 t.   Worcestershire sauce
1 t.   Cayenne pepper
1 t.   Salt

Sauté onions and celery in butter until onions are translucent, add flour, cook this roux about 5 minutes. Incorporate stock, simmer for 20 to 25 minutes. Add beer and cheddar cheese, allow cheese to melt.

Just before serving, add Half & Half, mustard, worcestershire sauce, cayenne, and salt.

Makes Ten Servings

Spinach Salad with Burgundy Dressing

Clean spinach and drain well, break into pieces and chill. Toss with dressing, and garnish with mushrooms and bacon bits.

Makes Four Servings

Combine all ingredients for dressing and chill.

SALAD:

4	Spinach, fresh, servings
1 c.	Mushrooms, fresh
1 c.	Bacon bits, freshly chopped

BURGUNDY DRESSING:

1 c.	Red wine vinegar
2 c.	Salad oil
2 t.	Sugar
1 t.	Salt
2 t.	Garlic, crushed
3/4 c.	Red Burgundy wine
1/2 t.	White pepper
2 t.	Worcestershire sauce
1/2 c.	Lemon juice, fresh

Marinated Salmon with Lime-Olive Oil Vinaigrette

Slice salmon thin, combine all ingredients for the marinade, and immerse salmon in marinade, and refrigerate 1 hour.

Drain salmon, arrange three slices on plate, garnish with baby lettuce. Arrange three small spoonfuls of caviar in front of salmon.

Combine ingredients for Herb Chantilly, mixing well. Nap sauce over end of salmon.

Makes Six Servings

1	Salmon fillet, 12 oz.

MARINADE:

2 oz.	Olive oil
1/2 ea.	Lime juice
1/4 ea.	Lemon juice
1/4 oz.	White wine vinegar
1 T.	Shallots, minced
1/2 T.	Pink peppercorns, cracked
4 oz.	White wine
1 T.	Chives, chopped

GARNISH:

6	Baby lettuce, portions
2 oz.	Salmon, sturgeon, and white fish caviar (each)

HERB CHANTILLY:

1/2 c.	Heavy cream, whipped
1 t.	Vinegar
1 t.	Mixed herbs, chopped
	Salt, pepper (to taste)

Catfish Topped with Crab Meat and Cornbread Crumbs

4 ea.	Catfish, 5 oz. portions
	Salt, pepper, lemon juice
	(to taste)
1/2 oz.	Butter
1 oz.	Onions, minced
4 oz.	Crabmeat
2 ea.	Shallots, minced
4 oz.	White wine
1 c.	Stock
2 oz.	Ham, julienne
1/2 c.	Cornbread crumbs
4 oz.	Bechamel, thick
1 oz.	Sherry
2 oz.	Butter
	Salt (to taste)

Sauté onions in butter until translucent, and add crabmeat.

Butter a shallow pan, sprinkle with shallots. Place catfish on top of shallots, add wine, stock, and ham. Cover with buttered paper, bring to a simmer in oven at 325 degrees. Poach catfish in 350-degree oven until done, about 5 to 10 minutes. Remove to warm platter.

Spread catfish with crabmeat mixture, sprinkle with cornbread crumbs, gratinee in broiler. Reduce poaching liquid until slightly thickened. Add Bechamel, reduce until sauce consistency. Flavor heavy cream with sherry, swirl in butter, and adjust salt. Serve catfish on a bed of sauce with ham.

Makes Four Servings

Fillet of Walleye Pike "Creek Style"

4 lbs.	Walleye Pike filets, fresh, 8 oz. each, skin removed
6 oz.	Butter
2 oz.	Shallots, finely chopped
8 oz.	Celery, leek, carrots, and mushrooms, peeled and cut into julienne strips
	Salt, white pepper (to taste)
12 oz.	Chablis
12 oz.	Fish stock
1 t.	Lemon juice
1 pt.	Whipping cream
6	Scallions, finely sliced

Butter a shallow pan, place shallots and vegetable strips over the bottom of pan. Place the filets over the vegetables. Sprinkle salt and pepper on top of filets. Add wine, fish stock, and lemon juice, then cover with foil. Bring to a boil on top of stove, then place in oven at 400 degrees and poach for 4 to 5 minutes. Remove the poached filets and place on a serving dish, keep warm.

Reduce the fish stock, add the whipping cream, and reduce again until creamy. With a wire whip, gradually work small pieces of butter into the sauce, add scallions, and adjust the seasoning. Pour over filets and serve.

Makes Eight Servings

Chicken Hunter-Style

Debone chicken, cut chicken into bite-sized pieces. Cut all vegetables into uniform pieces, leaving cherry tomatoes whole. Sauté chicken, add vegetables, and sauté 2 minutes. Add wine and soy sauce, cover, and simmer 5 minutes.

Serve with rice or noodles.

Makes Four Servings

1	Chicken, 2-1/2 lb.
1	Broccoli, bunch
1	Green pepper, chopped
1	Onion, small, chopped
8 oz.	Mushrooms, fresh, chopped
2	Carrots, chopped
2	Celery stems, chopped
2	Zucchinis, chopped
16	Cherry tomatoes, whole
4 oz.	White wine
4 oz.	Soy sauce

Emince of Beef a la Deutch

Heat oil until hot in a skillet, and sauté the beef just enough to brown. Remove the beef to a sauce pot. In the same skillet, sauté the peppers, mushrooms, and onions until almost done. Add the brown sauce and bring to a boil. Add the sliced beef, simmer for 35 to 40 minutes or until the beef is tender, then season.

Deep fry the potatoes and place on top of the beef at the time of serving.

Makes Six Servings

3 lbs.	Triangle Tip Beef, sliced in small thin strips
1/2 c.	Vegetable oil
3	Bell peppers, thinly sliced
1 lb.	Mushrooms, fresh, sliced
2 c.	Onions, sliced
2 qts.	Brown sauce
2 lbs.	Potatoes, sliced

1 c.	Yellow cornmeal
1/4 c.	Sugar, granulated
1/2 t.	Salt
1/4 t.	Baking soda
2	Eggs, large, beaten
1 c.	Dark molasses
2 oz.	Butter, soft
1/2 t.	Cinnamon, ground
1/4 t.	Ginger, ground
1/2 t.	Cloves, ground
6 c.	Hot milk

Mix together the cornmeal, sugar, salt, and baking soda. Add the beaten eggs, molasses, butter, and spices. Pour in 3 cups of hot milk and blend together. Pour the mixture into a 2-quart casserole that has been well buttered. Bake in oven at 325 degrees for 25 minutes or until hot.

Stir in the remaining 3 cups of hot milk, reduce oven temperature to 225 degrees and bake the pudding for 5 hours. Allow to stand for 30 minutes to set. Serve the pudding with whipped cream and sprinkle with ground ginger.

Makes One 2-Quart Casserole

The Cornish Influence

It is hard to imagine the English would not have an influence in the development of Rocky Mountain cuisine, but it's harder to determine a singular contribution. The answer is **"pasties"**.

The miners who came to the Rockies also came from the United Kingdom — principally Welshmen and Cornishmen. While many came via the mines of Minnesota, most were experienced miners. They knew it was exhausting work, and energy needed to be maintained. The miner's "main course" was the filled dough pastie. Today, you can still see miners stopping before their shift for breakfast at the local cafe and buying a pie on the way out, to nourish them underground.

Mix flour and salt, cut in shortening, and mix to resemble medium coarse crumbs. Sprinkle water one tablespoon at a time, mix with fork until it forms cohesive dough. Shape into smooth ball with floured hands. DO NOT KNEAD. Roll dough 1/8-inch thick. Cut out 5-inch circles with round cutter. Fill with Pork or Grandmother's Pasty Filling.

3 c.	Flour, sifted
1/2 t.	Salt
1-1/4 c.	Solid vegetable shortening
6 - 7 T.	Cold water

Mix all ingredients and place 3 T. of mixture on half of each pasty circle. Fold and seal each circle. Bake in oven at 325 degrees for approximately 45 minutes.

PORK PASTY FILLING:

1	Baking potato, small, cut in 1/4-inch cubes
2	Onions, small, finely chopped
1/2 t.	Salt
1/4 t.	Dried sage, crumbled
1/4 t.	Pepper, freshly ground
1/2 lb.	Pork Shoulder, boneless, trimmed and cut in 1/4-inch cubes

Mix all, except butter. Place 3 T. of mixture on half of each pasty circle. Top each with 1 t. of butter. Fold and seal each circle. Bake in oven at 325 degrees for approximately 45 minutes.

Makes Sixteen Pasties

GRANDMOTHER'S PASTY FILLING:

1/2 lb.	Top Round Steak, cut in 1/4-inch cubes
1	Baking potato, small, cut in 1/4-inch cubes
3/4 c.	Carrots, 1/4-inch cubes
2	Onions, small, finely chopped
2	Bacon slices, cooked crisp and crumbled
3 T.	Parsley, fresh, minced
1 t.	Salt
1/4 t.	Pepper, freshly ground
5 T.+1 t.	Butter, unsalted

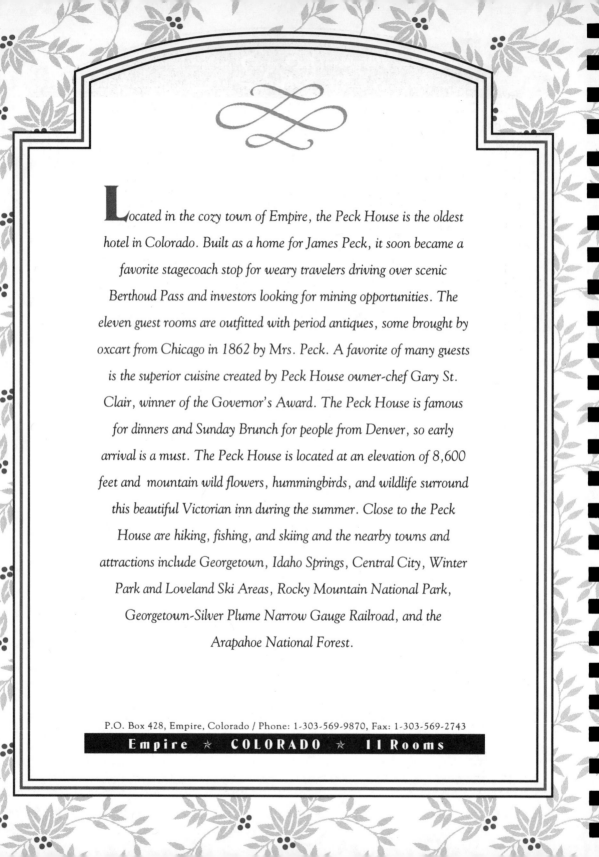

*L*ocated in the cozy town of Empire, the Peck House is the oldest hotel in Colorado. Built as a home for James Peck, it soon became a favorite stagecoach stop for weary travelers driving over scenic Berthoud Pass and investors looking for mining opportunities. The eleven guest rooms are outfitted with period antiques, some brought by oxcart from Chicago in 1862 by Mrs. Peck. A favorite of many guests is the superior cuisine created by Peck House owner-chef Gary St. Clair, winner of the Governor's Award. The Peck House is famous for dinners and Sunday Brunch for people from Denver, so early arrival is a must. The Peck House is located at an elevation of 8,600 feet and mountain wild flowers, hummingbirds, and wildlife surround this beautiful Victorian inn during the summer. Close to the Peck House are hiking, fishing, and skiing and the nearby towns and attractions include Georgetown, Idaho Springs, Central City, Winter Park and Loveland Ski Areas, Rocky Mountain National Park, Georgetown-Silver Plume Narrow Gauge Railroad, and the Arapahoe National Forest.

P.O. Box 428, Empire, Colorado / Phone: 1-303-569-9870, Fax: 1-303-569-2743

Empire ✲ COLORADO ✲ 11 Rooms

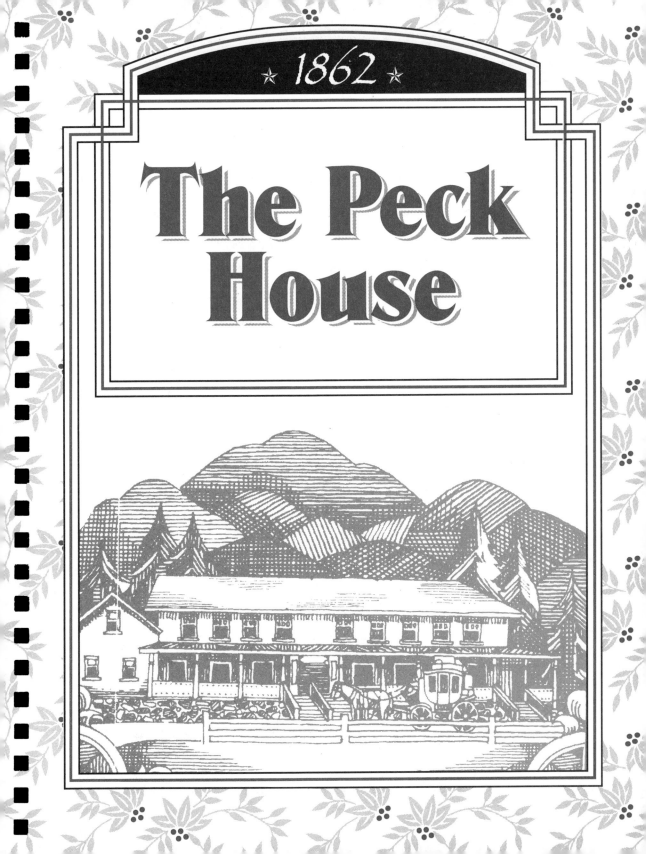

Cranberry-Orange Chutney

4 c. Cranberries, fresh
4 c. Water
1/2 c. Orange juice concentrate
3 c. Sugar
1 t. Cinnamon, ground cloves,
ground allspice, mace,
nutmeg (each)
1/2 t. Ginger, ground
1/4 t. Cayenne pepper
1/4 c. Golden raisins
1/2 c. Red bell pepper, julienned
Zest Orange

Combine all ingredients in a stainless steel saucepan. Simmer until reduced by half. This may take several hours. Stir occasionally. Serve as an accompaniment to meats, fowl, fish or pâtés.

Makes Two Quarts

Five Onion French Onion Soup

6 Garlic cloves, peeled
2 c. Yellow onions
2 Leek, whites only
1 c. Shallots
3 T. Olive oil
1/2 t. Thyme
1/4 t. Black pepper, ground
4 c. Rich beef stock
1 c. Chicken stock
6 Scallions, chopped
2 c. White Bermuda onions,
thinly sliced

Swiss cheese
Croutons

Mix together in a bowl, the garlic, yellow onions, leeks, shallots, olive oil, thyme, pepper, and enough stock to blend until smooth. Add the blended mixture to the rest of the stock and pour into a stock pot. Add the scallions and white onions. Simmer two hours, and salt to taste.

Garnish with sliced swiss cheese and croutons.

Makes Four Servings

Mango Chutney Salad Dressing

Blend all of the ingredients together until smooth. In a large bowl, mix together blended ingredients with mayonnaise and sour cream. It's now ready to serve. This dressing is perfect for the Green and Gold Salad (see recipe below) or a fresh fruit salad.

Makes One Cup

1/4 c.	Major Grey's Chutney
Pinch	Salt
Dash	Tabasco
3 T.	Salad oil
1/8 t.	Curry powder
3 t.	Red wine vinegar
1/2 c.	Mayonnaise
1/2 c.	Sour cream

Green and Gold Salad

Fill a bowl with a mixture of lettuce, greens, spinach. Add the remaining ingredients and serve with chutney dressing.

Makes One Serving

	Lettuce, greens, spinach
1/2	Avocado, sliced
4 oz.	Mandarin oranges
1/2	Banana, sliced
2 oz.	Chutney dressing

Shrimp Sarah

Cook the mushrooms, raisins, chutney, spices, worcestershire sauce, and cream in a small skillet over medium heat for 5 minutes, or until thickened. Arrange the shrimp on four skewers. Brush the shrimp with a little melted butter, oil, or margarine. Broil 4 to 5 inches from heat for 4 to 5 minutes, turning once, or until cooked.

Serve on rice with sauce.

Makes Four Servings

1/4 c.	Mushrooms, sliced
3 T.	Golden raisins
2 T.	Major Grey's chutney (heaping tablespoon)
1/4 t.	Curry powder
Dash	Cayenne pepper
Dash	Worcestershire sauce
1/2 c.	Heavy cream
20	Shrimp, large, shelled and deveined
	Butter, melted, oil, or margarine
3 c.	Long grain and wild rice, cooked (1 c. uncooked)

Hot Buttered Rum Mix

RUM MIXTURE:
- 1/2 lb. Brown sugar
- 1/3 lb. Margarine
- 1-1/2 T. Honey
- 1/4 t. Vanilla
- 1/4 t. Nutmeg, cinnamon (each)
- 1 Cinnamon stick
- 1-1/2 oz. White rum
  Boiling water

Mix brown sugar, margarine, honey, vanilla, nutmeg, and cinnamon together well.

Place one heaping T. of rum mixture in a warm pre-rinsed mug and add 1 to 1-1/2 oz. white rum. Fill the mug with boiling water.

Stir vigorously with a cinnamon stick.

Makes One Serving

Sour Cream Coffee Cake

- 1/2 c. Shortening or oil
- 1 c. Sugar
- 1 c. Sour cream
- 2 Eggs
- 1 t. Vanilla
- 2 c. Flour
- 1 t. Baking powder
- 1 t. Baking soda
- 1/4 t. Salt
- 1 T. Mayonnaise (for high altitude adjustment only, above 6,000 ft.)

TOPPING:
- 1/3 c. Almonds
- 1 t. Cinnamon
- 1/4 c. Brown sugar
  Jam (your favorite)

Cream together shortening, sugar, and sour cream. Add eggs and the rest of the ingredients, and mayonnaise, if necessary. Pour half of the batter in a greased 9 x 13-inch cake pan. Mix the almonds, cinnamon, and brown sugar and sprinkle half of the topping on top. Add the remaining batter.

Swirl a few tablespoons of your favorite jam into the batter lightly. Add the rest of the topping on top of the cake.

Bake in 350-degree oven for 40 to 55 minutes or until done.

(For low-fat substitutes: use yogurt instead of sour cream, Canola oil instead of shortening.)

Makes Twenty Servings

Ice Box Ginger Muffins

Cream sugar and shortening. Add beaten egg yolks. Add baking soda and spices to the molasses and then to the mixture. Alternating, add milk and flour. Fold in beaten egg whites. Add raisins and nuts, and add mayonnaise, if necessary. Put in the refrigerator. Use the batter without stirring. Lightly grease miniature muffin pans.

Bake at 350 degrees for 15 minutes. This batter will keep in the refrigerator for a very long time.

Makes About 60 Small Muffins

1 c.	Brown sugar
1 c.	Shortening
4	Egg yolks, beaten
1 c.	Molasses
2 t.	Baking soda
1 t.	Cinnamon
1/2 t.	Ginger
1/4 t.	Allspice
1 c.	Buttermilk
4 c.	Flour
4	Egg whites, beaten
1/2 c.	Raisins
1 c.	Nuts
1 T.	Mayonnaise (for high altitude adjustment only, above 6,000 ft.)

Smoked Colorado Corn Chowder

Cut the kernels off of the corn. Place the corn on an ovenproof dish and place it in a meat smoker for 15 minutes in a heavy alderwood smoke. Thicken the hot milk with the flour. Cook for 10 minutes. Sauté the celery leaf in a small amount of butter. Add all of the ingredients, including the smoked corn, to the milk and flour. Cook the chowder in a double boiler for at least 1 hour before serving.

Makes Four Servings

4 ears	Colorado sweet corn, fresh
1 qt.	Hot milk
1/4 c.	Flour
2 c.	Potatoes, cooked, 1/4-inch dice
1/4 c.	Celery leaf, chopped
1/4 c.	Bacon, crisp, finely chopped
1/4 t.	Black pepper, fresh ground

Colorado Fall Pheasant

BUFFALO SAUSAGE:

1 lb.	Ground Buffalo
1/2 t.	Salt
1/2 t.	Black pepper
1/2 t.	Garlic, granulated
1/4 t.	Marjoram
4	Pheasant breasts, 6-7 oz. each, boneless, skinless

PEACH AND PORT SAUCE:

1 c.	Port
1 c.	Sugar
4	Colorado peaches, peeled and sliced

Thoroughly mix all ingredients for the sausage. Refrigerate overnight.

Reduce the port and sugar to half its volume over medium-high heat. Add the peaches. Gently simmer for 1 hour.

Gently flatten each pheasant breast with a meat mallet into a rectangle shape of 6 x 8-inches. By hand, roll out 1/4 lb. of sausage in a tube shape about 6-inches long. Roll the pheasant breast around the sausage firmly. You should end up with a tube that is 6-inches long x 2-inches in diameter. Repeat this for each pheasant breast.

Bake the pheasant in 350-degree oven for 30 minutes. Slice into 3/4-inch wheel shapes.

TO SERVE: Arrange on a plate and top with the hot peach and port sauce.

Makes Four Servings

Colorado Mountain Bass Macadamia

1	Durango Striped Bass, filet, skinless, boneless
1 part	Brown sugar
1 part	Lime juice, fresh
2 t.	Macadamia nuts, chopped

Place fish filet(s) on a well-butered sheet pan. Cook for 10 minutes in 450-degree oven. Take the filets from the oven and brush with a sauce of equal parts brown sugar and lime juice. Garnish each filet with macadamia nuts. Return to the oven for 2 minutes and serve.

Makes One Serving

Colorado Lamb Dijon

Mix the glaze ingredients together thoroughly. Thoroughly trim the lamb so that there is no fat, no gristle, or membrane.

Grill the lamb over a fairly hot flame to no more than medium rare. While grilling, brush the lamb generously with the Herbed-Dijon Glaze.

Makes Eight Servings

8   Lamb loin eye, boneless
    (finished product of 6-8 oz.)

HERBED-DIJON GLAZE:
1/2 c.   Honey
1/2 c.   Grey Poupon Dijon Mustard
1/4 t.   Powdered ginger
1/4 t.   Worcestershire sauce
1/4 t.   Parlsey flakes, dried
1/4 t.   Chives, chopped
1/4 t.   Garlic, granulated

The Basque Influence

The Basque people have long been considered some of the best sheepherders of the Rockies, probably due to their experience in the similar terrain of the Pyrennes of southern France and northern Spain. The Basque cuisine's influences are strongest in the central and northern Rockies — Colorado, Wyoming, Idaho, and Montana. Most of the domestic lamb comes from these states.

Colorado Gold Sundae

Simmer the Colorado peaches and sugar together for 1 hour and then chill for later use. Blend in a blender 1/2 c. of the chilled, cooked peaches with the B & B, peach brandy, cloves, and ice cream. Refrigerate overnight. Divide the blended mixture into four large, tall wine glasses. Top it with the remaining cooked peaches and a touch of whipped cream. Watch Out!

Makes Two Servings

4   Colorado peaches, fresh,
    peeled and sliced
1 c.   Sugar
2 oz.   B & B
2 oz.   Peach brandy
1/4 t.   Cloves, ground
1 pt.   French Vanilla ice cream
    Whipped cream

Midway between Aspen and Glenwood Springs is the village of Redstone and the Historic Redstone Inn. The Inn's 35 guestrooms and suites are highlighted with antiques and many personal touches, with spectacular mountain views as a part of each room's decoration. Renowned for excellent dining, the gracious Redstone Room with its Rocky Mountain cuisine, is a valley favorite. The new Bar and Deck offers a friendly spot to have a grilled burger, swordfish, flavorful soup, garden salad, or hearty breakfast. TVs, phones, year-round swimming pool, hot tub, health club, tennis court, and full-service banquet and meeting room facilities are only a part of the Redstone's numerous amenities. Pristine mountain air awaits the sports-minded traveler on the Redstone Inn's 22-acre site with sleigh rides and cross-country skiing in the winter months, and horseback riding, hiking, trout fishing, and tennis in the summer months. There are year-round shops, galleries, and historic sites, and nearby is the Colorado National Monument and Black Canyon of the Gunnison National Monument.

0082 Redstone Blvd., Redstone, CO / Phone: 1-303-963-2526, 1-800-748-2524, Fax: 1-303-963-2526

Redstone ☆ COLORADO ☆ 35 Rooms

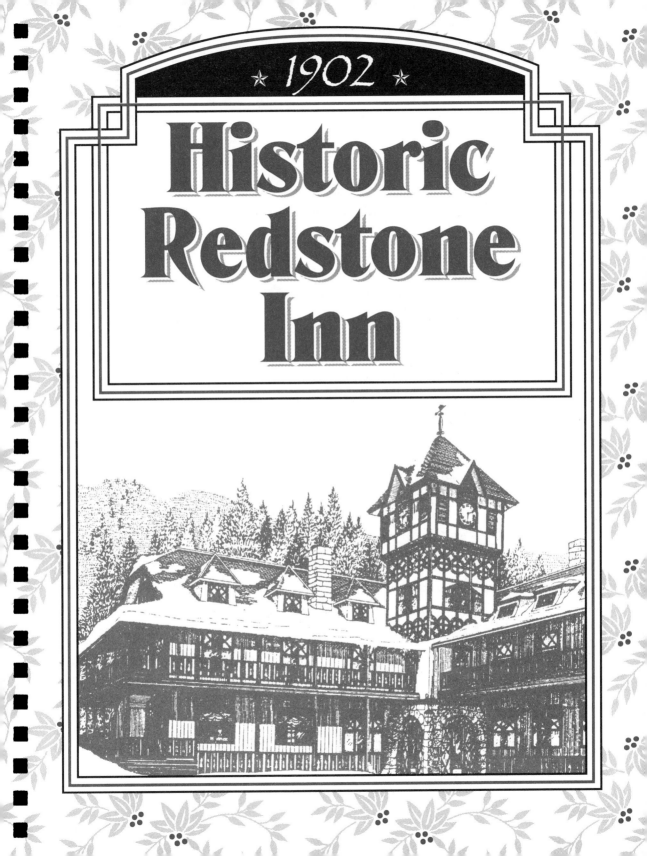

✶ 1902 ✶

Historic
Redstone
Inn

Crab Wontons with Honey-Mustard Sauce

1/2 lb.	Lump crabmeat, diced fine
5 oz.	Cream cheese, low-fat, room temperature to soften
2	Green onions, finely sliced
1 t.	Soy sauce
3 T.	Mayonnaise
6	Egg roll skins
3	Eggs, beaten
2 c.	Oil for deep frying
	Cornmeal

HONEY-MUSTARD SAUCE:

1 c.	Honey
1/3 c.	Orange juice
1/3 c.	Dijon mustard

Mix crabmeat, cream cheese, onions, soy sauce, and mayonnaise in mixer completely.

Layout two egg roll skins on a cutting surface, brush with beaten eggs lightly to cover. Cut each in four equal squares. Work quickly as skins will dry out. Place a teaspoon of mixture on each square. Bring up opposite corners of the skin to the center and pinch to seal in the crab. Be sure to seal securely. Set on a tray dusted with cornmeal to prevent sticking. Finish remainder in the same fashion. Let rest in refrigerator at least 1 hour to dry.

Heat oil, of your choice, for deep frying at 350 degrees. Submerge a few wontons at a time cooking until golden brown, about 60 seconds. Drain. Keep warm until serving.

Combine honey, orange juice, and Dijon mustard and warm.

Makes 24 Wontons

Colorado White Chili

1	Stewing chicken, 3-lb. Onions, carrots, celery (each, rough cut)
1 lb.	Great Northern beans, soaked overnight
3 c.	White onions, diced
1-1/2 t.	Garlic, fresh minced
1-1/2 T.	Cumin
	Cayenne pepper (to taste)
	Chicken bouillon cubes
1	Green chiles, chopped (27-oz. can)
	Salt, pepper (to taste)
1 lb.	Jalapeño Jack cheese, sliced thinly
	Tortilla Chips

Cover with water and cook chicken in large pot with mire poix (onion, carrot, celery, rough cut for flavor), approx. 45 minutes. Drain, discard veggies, and reserve stock. Debone when cool and chop coarsely.

In a large pot, cook drained beans, until tender in chicken stock (approx. 45 minutes).

In a separate large pot, sauté onions in garlic with a little chicken fat skimmed from chicken stock; add spices and bouillon cubes, if necessary, to fortify chicken flavor. Rinse and drain chiles, add to sautéed spice mixture; add cooked beans with broth, chopped chicken, and season with salt and pepper to taste. Add water, if necessary.

Melt Jalapeño Jack cheese on top of each bowl. Garnish with tortilla chips.

Makes Eight Servings

Redstone Smoked Trout

Prepare the smoking marinade — 1 c. vegetable oil, well seasoned with salt and pepper. Marinate trout 20 minutes before smoking.

Light small pile of charcoal briquettes in smoker. When coals are grey, add two handfuls of wet hickory chips directly over the grey coals. Fill drip pan with ice to reduce direct heat on grill. Position grill on top of drip pan; lay out marinated trout on the grill with skin side down. Cover smoker and watch for smoke to billow.

After 35 minutes, check for doneness, examining trout for caramel-brown color. They are done when they are nicely browned. Remove very carefully with large spatula and transfer to tray or plate to cool.

Serve with horseradish cream, capers, and chopped red onions.

Makes Four Servings

1	Upright, domestic smoker (we use a charcoal briquette fired one)
2 lb.	Hickory chips, soaked in water
5 lbs.	Charcoal briquettes
4	Trout, 8-oz., boned and butterflied

MARINADE:
1 c.	Vegetable oil
	Salt, pepper (to taste)

HORSERADISH CREAM:
4 parts	Sour cream
1 part	Prepared horseradish Worcestershire sauce (to taste)
	Capers
	Red onions, chopped

Tuna au Poivre on Field Greens

Combine mayonnaise, honey, and cinnamon to make á la minute dressing.

Arrange greens on large, chilled plates. Place mango slices around perimeter of greens.

In a sauté pan or on your charcoal grill, cook tuna steak medium-rare and let rest on a cutting board for 2 minutes. Slice tuna steaks into fingers and arrange over dressed greens.

Makes Four Servings

1 c.	Mayonnaise, low-cholesterol
1/4 c.	Honey
1 t.	Cinnamon
2 lb.	Assorted fresh greens of your choice (we use baby romaine, red leaf, baby spinach, radicchio and bib)
4 ea.	Mahi or tuna steaks, 6-oz., rubbed with cracked black peppercorns
2 ea.	Mangos, fresh, peeled and sliced lengthwise

Sea Scallops with Linguini and Roasted Red Pepper Sauce

Bell peppers
1/4 c.   Shallots, finely diced
1 t.   Garlic, minced
1 c.   Chicken stock
1 t.   Tomato paste
1 T.   Olive oil
1-1/2 lb.   Sea scallops, fresh

6 c.   Linguini, cooked
Basil leaves, fresh

Char peppers by roasting them directly on gas flame stove top or on an outdoor BBQ, until *entirely* black. Immediately, wrap in plastic bag or plastic wrap for 5 minutes to steam. Remove charred peppers and rinse under cold water, charred skins will easily rub off. Remove the core and seeds from the bell peppers.

Blend shallots, garlic, chicken stock, and tomato paste in blender with the bell pepper until puréed. Warm in small saucepan and hold.

In hot, non-stick pan, heat olive oil and add one-third of scallops and sear until golden brown on each side. Remove and keep warm. Repeat with remaining two batches by carefully browning and not burning.

Heat pasta, laddle on the sauce, and top with seared scallops. Garnish with fresh basil leaves.

Makes Six Servings

Tiramisu

This sinful dessert pays tribute to the Italian stone workers brought over to help quarry the famous Colorado Yule marble from just down the road from the Inn.

32 ea.   Lady fingers
5 c.   Espresso
10   Eggs, separated
10 T.   White sugar
1 lb.   Marscapone cheese
2 c.   Heavy cream
3 T.   Cocoa powder

Dip 16 lady fingers in espresso quickly and line a 12 x 9 x 2-inch dessert dish. Beat yolks with sugar until frothy. Beat whites separately until stiff and fold into yolk mixture, mix in Marscapone cheese and wine. Separately whip cream, until stiff and fold into Marscapone mixture, until smooth.

Pour 1/2 mixture on top of lady fingers. Dip remaining fingers into espresso and layer them neatly in dish. Finish with layer of remaining Marscapone mixture, smoothed neatly on top and lightly dust with cocoa.

Chill at least six hours before serving. A decadent experience!

Makes Twelve Servings

Pineapple-Cream Cheese Baklava

Preheat oven to 375 degrees. Mix cream cheese, ricotta, yolks, sugar, pineapple, vanilla, and salt together thoroughly.

Place one sheet of phyllo into pan and lightly brush with the warmed butter. Repeat 12 times. Pour cheese mixture evenly onto stacked sheets. Top with the remaining phyllo, buttering in the same manner.

With sharp knife, score baklava into 24 squares (for bite sized pieces, cut each square into two triangles). Bake in the preheated oven for 35 to 40 minutes until golden brown.

Combine ingredients in saucepan and simmer for 15 minutes stirring to keep in solution. Pour warmed sauce over entire baked pastry. Allow 2 hours to cool and set. Cut pieces and serve.

Makes Twenty-Four Servings

1 lb.	Cream cheese, low-fat
1 lb.	Ricotta cheese
4 ea.	Egg yolks
1/2 c.	Pineapple, crushed, drained, reserving juice
1 t.	Vanilla
1/2 t.	Salt
1 lb.	Phyllo dough sheets
1-1/2 c.	Clarified butter
1	Jelly roll pan, 12 x 17-inch

SYRUP FOR BAKED PASTRY:

1 c.	Sugar
1 c.	Honey
1	Cinnamon stick
Zest	Lemon
1 c.	Water

Redstone Colada

Blend well. Top with whipped cream dollop, drizzled with grenadine.

Garnish with a fresh strawberry.

Makes One Serving

1/2 oz.	Banana liqueur
1/2 oz.	Coconut rum
2 oz.	Half & Half
1/2 c.	Strawberries (fresh or frozen)
2	Scoops of ice cubes
	Whipped cream
	Grenadine
	Strawberries, fresh, whole

Built by F. O. Stanley, co-inventor of the Stanley Steamer automobile, the historic Stanley Hotel is high in the Rockies in Estes Park, Colorado. It is known world-wide for its white-columned Georgian architecture and magnificent views of Longs Peak and the Continental Divide. There is a heated outdoor pool, Jacuzzi, spacious lawn for croquet, and three restaurants. Brides regularly descend the hotel's grand staircase to marry on the front lawn. This beautiful hotel offers conference rooms with mountain views framed in arched windows. Concert, theatre, and dance programs are performed year-round. Steam cars still make annual pilgrimages up the canyon to the Gateway to Rocky Mountain National Park. The area boasts miles of trails for hiking and cross-country skiing, excellent golf courses, fishing, and horseback riding. There is a music festival in the summer. While you are there, take a drive on Trail Ridge Road, the highest continuous road in America, which crosses the tundra high above Estes Park.

P.O. Box 1767, Estes Park, CO / Phone: 1-303-586-3371, 1-800-ROCKIES, Fax: 1-303-586-3673

Estes Park ✴ COLORADO ✴ 92 Rooms

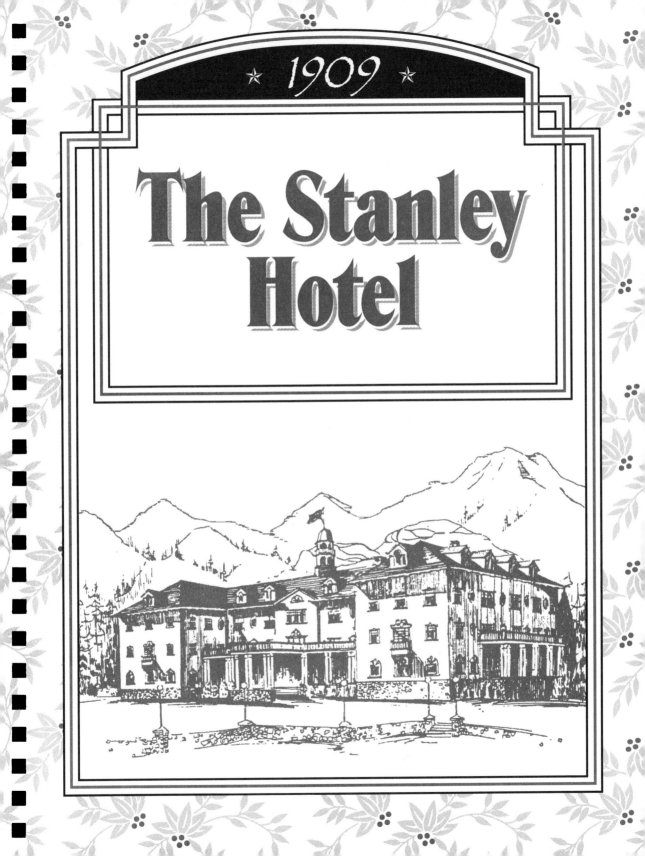

Green Chili & Red Bean Soup

4 c.	Red beans
1 can	Green chilis
1	Yellow onion, medium
1	Green pepper, medium
1	Red bell pepper, medium
1/4 c.	Olive oil
1/2 gal.	Chicken stock
1/4 c.	Parsley
1/8 c.	Garlic, chopped fine
1/2 oz.	Tabasco
2/3 t.	Chili powder
1/2 t.	Cumin, garlic (granulated), basil (dried)
1/4 t.	White pepper
1/8 t.	Cayenne
	Corn tortillas

Soak red beans overnight in cold water. Dice all vegetables. Chop garlic fine. Sauté vegetables in olive oil, until onions are transparent. Add chicken stock and remaining ingredients.

Simmer for 2 hours. Cool properly and hold in refrigerator for no longer than 7 days.

TO SERVE: Reheat soup to 180 degrees. Serve with fried corn tortilla chips.

Makes One Gallon

Southwestern Black Bean Salad

2	Black beans (2-lb. cans)
1/4 c.	Olive oil
2-1/2 T.	Red wine vinegar
1/2 t.	Salt
1/4 t.	Pepper
1/2 t.	Cumin, ground
1/4 c.	Parsley, chopped
1/2	Red onion, chopped
1/2 c.	Celery, sliced
1/2 c.	Black olives, sliced
1/2 c.	Corn

Rinse beans in cold water and drain. Combine olive oil, red wine vinegar, salt, pepper, cumin, parsley, and toss with beans and vegetables. Can be made a day ahead, but bring to room temperature.

Makes Eight Servings

Beans

When speaking of beans on the frontier, invariably one first remembers the scene from Blazing Saddles around the campfire. Long a staple on the frontier, beans were easily transportable and did not spoil. Before European settlement, Native Americans also valued beans for these same qualities. One such native bean is the pinto, much in use today, appearing in southwestern cooking as the refried bean. Carolyn Niethammer, in her book *American Indian Food and Lore*, writes about the tepary bean, grown by Native Americans for centuries:

"The Spaniards found the Papagos growing teparies in 1699. The Indians called the native bean 'pawi,' and it was one of their staples.

In fact, it was so common in their diet that they were called the 'Bean People.' Apparently when the Spaniards asked the Papagos what they called this food, they answered "t'pawi" (It is a bean) and the Spaniards corrupted this to tepary."

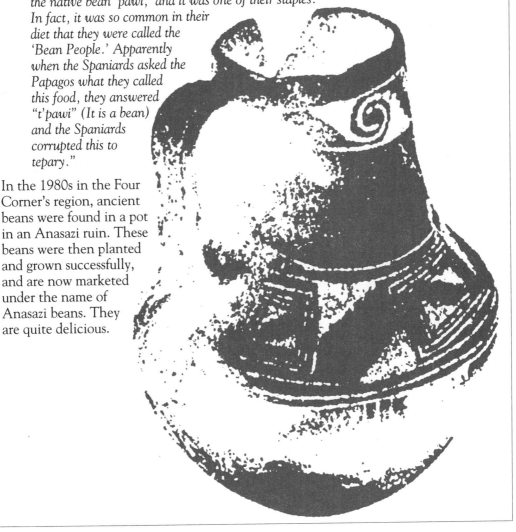

In the 1980s in the Four Corner's region, ancient beans were found in a pot in an Anasazi ruin. These beans were then planted and grown successfully, and are now marketed under the name of Anasazi beans. They are quite delicious.

Cranberry Apple Relish

1 c. Cranberries, fresh or frozen
1 c. Red Delicious apples, peeled and chopped (about 1 large one)
1/2 c. Raisins
1 c. Apple juice concentrate, unsweetened, frozen, defrosted
1/2 t. Lemon juice, fresh
1/2 t. Cinnamon, ground
1/8 t. Ginger, ground

Put all ingredients, except cinnamon and ginger, in a saucepan and bring to a boil. Reduce heat and simmer, partially covered, for about 20 minutes or until cranberries have popped and sauce has thickened.

Remove from heat and stir in cinnamon and ginger. Refrigerate.

Makes Two Cups

Bishop's Bread

1-1/2 c. Flour
1-1/2 t. Baking powder
1/4 t. Salt
2/3 c. Chocolate chips
2 c. Walnuts, coarsely chopped
1 c. Dates, finely snipped
1 c. Glaced cherries, halved
3 Eggs
1 c. Granulated sugar

Sift flour, baking powder, and salt in medium bowl. Stir in chocolate chips, walnuts, dates, and cherries until will coated.

In large bowl, mixer at medium speed, beat eggs well; gradually beat in sugar. Fold in flour mixture. Pour into 10 x 5 x 3-inch loaf pan. Bake 1-1/2 hours at 325 degrees. Wrap in foil and store in refrigerator or freeze.

Makes One Loaf

Chicken Andouille

Julienne chicken breast. Slice sausage on the bias. Lightly flour chicken. Heat olive oil in sauté pan. Add chicken and sausage to the pan. Sauté until chicken is almost cooked. Add chopped garlic and tomato-basil sauce. Let simmer for 2 minutes. Add cream and garlic butter.

Boil or reheat tortellini. Spread tortellini evenly around the center of the plate. Arrange chicken strips like bicycle spokes over the tortellini. Place the sausage between the spokes and pour the sauce over everything. Garnish with chopped parsley and Parmesan cheese, as you wish.

Makes One Serving

1	Chicken breast, 6-oz.
4 oz.	Andouille sausage (not italian)
1 T.	Olive oil
1 t.	Garlic, chopped
4 oz.	Tomato-basil sauce
2 oz.	Cream
2 oz.	Garlic butter (may be purchased in the dairy section of your market)
6 oz.	Cheese tortellini
Pinch	Parsley, chopped
1 oz.	Parmesan cheese

Shrimp Etouffee

From Patricia Maher, The Stanley's Public Relations and Fine Arts Manager and Managing Director of The Stanley Historic Trust. She won the Estes Park Trail Gazette's Yearly Cooking Contest with this recipe.

Peel shrimp, reserving the peelings. Simmer peelings in water for 15 minutes. Drain, reserving shrimp stock. Heat oil. Sauté onions, green pepper, and celery for 5-8 minutes. Add roux* and salt. Slowly add 1 c. of shrimp stock at a time, mixing thoroughly after each of the approximately four cups.

Add garlic, red pepper, and thyme. Simmer 30 to 40 minutes, stirring occasionally, until thick. Add shrimp, green onions, and parsley. Simmer 7 to 10 minutes, until shrimp turns pink. Adjust seasonings as you please. Serve over hot rice.

*Make roux with equal parts white flour and butter (or whole wheat flour and olive oil). Heat the butter, then blend in the flour by constantly stirring with a whisk. Use a heavy cast iron skillet over a low flame. Stir and cook long enough to remove the raw flour taste, a minimum of 5 minutes, until the color is light brown.

Makes Four to Five Servings

1 lb.	Shrimp, reserve peelings
4 c.	Water
1 T.	Extra virgin olive oil or sesame oil
2	Onions, thinly sliced
1 c.	Green bell pepper, diced
2	Celery, large stalks, diced
1/2 c.	Roux
3 t.	Salt
1-2	Garlic cloves, minced
1 c.	Red bell pepper, finely diced
1 t.	Thyme, fresh, chopped (optional)
1 c.	Green onions, sliced
1 c.	Parsley, finely chopped

Pecan-Mushroom Vegetarian Spaghetti Sauce

1   Onion, chopped
1   Garlic clove, good-sized, pressed
1 c. Mushrooms, fresh, sliced
1   Green pepper, chopped
1 t. Kelp
1 t. Oregano
1/2 t. Basil
1/4 t. Cayenne
    Sea salt (to taste)
1-2 T. Olive oil
1   Tomato purée (2-lb. can)
1   Tomato paste (6-oz. can)
1   Bay leaf
1/2 c. Pecans, chopped

Artichoke or buckwheat spaghetti noodles

Warm the onion, garlic, mushrooms, green pepper, and seasonings (except bay leaf) in the oil. Add the tomato purée, tomato paste, and bay leaf. Bring to a boil and simmer for 5 minutes. Add pecans and serve over cooked noodles.

Makes Six to Eight Servings

Salmon Oscar Phyllo

1   Salmon filet, 7 oz., fresh
Pinch Lemon pepper
1 oz. Butter patty
3   Asparagus spears
2 oz. Alaskan crab leg meat
1   Phyllo pastry sheet
    Melted butter
    Bread crumbs

1   Lemon wedge
2 oz. Hollandaise sauce
    Parsley, chopped
    Paprika

Season salmon filet with lemon pepper. Place butter patty on salmon, then layer asparagus and crabmeat. Place the salmon in the top center of the phyllo sheet. Fold edges over the salmon lengthwise. Roll salmon in the phyllo sheet. Drizzle melted butter over the salmon. Sprinkle with bread crumbs. Bake at 375 degrees for 12 to 15 minutes (brush salmon with a little water to keep pastry from getting too brown).

To Serve: Top with Hollandaise sauce and lemon wedge. Garnish with chopped parsley and paprika.

Makes One Serving

F. O. Stanley's Mulled Cider

Combine the apple juice, grape juice, cranberry juice, orange juice concentrate, bay leaves, cinnamon, star anise, and cardamom in a 2-quart saucepan.

Heat until liquid just barely comes to a simmer. Do not let the cider boil or even begin to bubble. Heat for 45 minutes. Strain and serve warm.

NOTE: To double the recipe, double all ingredients except bay leaves. Increase them to four leaves.

Makes Five Cups

2 c.	Apple juice
2 c.	White grape juice
1 c.	Cranberry juice
1 T.	Orange juice concentrate
3	Bay leaves
1	Cinnamon stick, 3-inch
1	Point of star anise
2	Seeds of cardamom pods

Dandelion Wine

The late Ralph Baker's secret recipe. "Use your imagination. There is always a use for weeds! A day of work in the summertime will make a long winter a bit warmer."

Pick over the flowers and remove any stem ends. Put the flowers into a large warm crock. Pour the boiling water over them. Let stand for a week.

Strain, squeezing all of the juice out of the flowers. Throw the flowers away. Add the honey and stir well. Add the lemons, oranges and cloves. Stir. Soften the yeast in 1/2 c. of warm water and add to the mixture. Cover. Let stand for two more weeks.

Strain again and pour into your favorite bottles. Let stand, capped or uncorked, for five days. Cap or cork the bottles, and leave for at least two months. The longer, the stronger.

Makes Four Gallons

4 gal.	Dandelion flowerheads
4 gal.	Water, boiling
4 lbs.	Honey
2 T.	Yeast, softened
1/2 c.	Water, warm
4	Lemons, sliced
2	Oranges, sliced
12	Cloves, whole

Journalist John Day wrote of Durango's historic centerpiece: "It is the finest Victorian hotel in the state, and possibly in the West." Built in 1887 of native red brick and hand-carved sandstone, the Strater is an impressive example of American Victorian architecture. The hotel is appointed throughout with authentic walnut antiques and is fully renovated to include modern conveniences. The Strater's two dining rooms, the Columbian Room and Henry's Restaurant, offer traditional favorites and local specialties of the Rocky Mountains in a charming atmosphere, including exceptional Sunday Brunch. Live ragtime piano makes the Diamond Belle Saloon a popular gathering place. The Diamond Circle Theatre presents nightly melodramas in the summer, and there are convention and catering facilities. The hotel is just steps to shopping, the historic district, and Narrow Gauge Railroad. Nearby is the famed Mesa Verde National Park. Seasonal events include the Opera, Colorfest, and Snowdown. And for the sports enthusiast, there is hiking, horseback riding, tennis, and downhill and cross-country skiing.

699 Main Ave., Durango, CO / Phone: 1-303-247-4431, 1-800-247-4431, Fax: 1-303-259-2208

Durango ☆ **COLORADO** ☆ **93 Rooms**

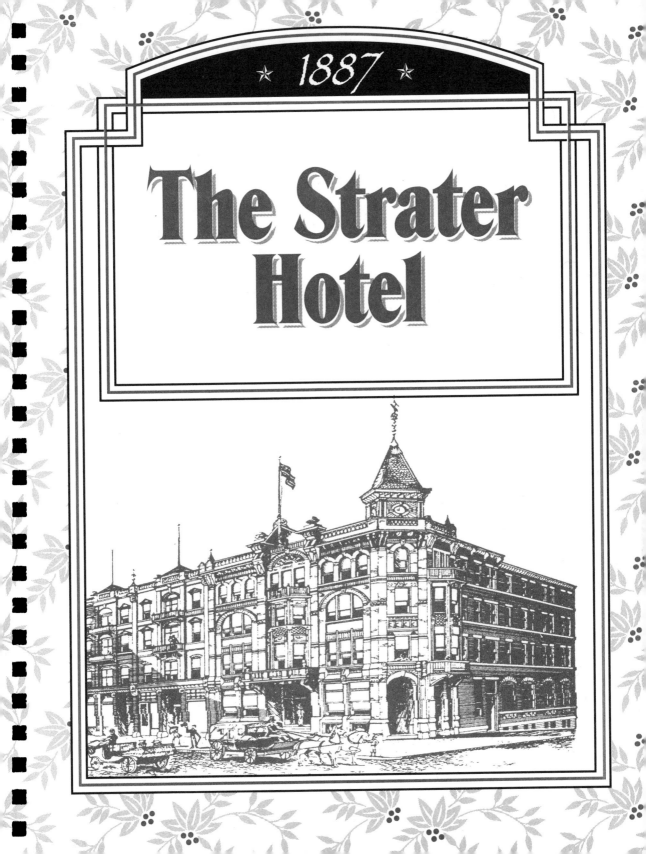

Black Bean and Chorizo Soup

1 c. Black beans, dry
5 qts. Water
10 oz. Chorizo (Mexican sausage), cooked
1-1/2 T. Chicken base
2 T. Cilantro, fresh, finely chopped
6 T. Roux (equal amounts flour and butter, cooked slightly)
1/2 c. Heavy cream

Combine beans and 2 quarts of water, boil 45 minutes, purée chorizo, and add to beans. Boil an additional 30 minutes. Set aside, cool slightly. Purée chorizo and bean mixture, strain. Save the bean mixture and liquid, separately.

Heat the strained liquid with 3 quarts of water, add chicken base and cilantro, bring to a boil and add roux. Mix until dissolved. Strain again and add this liquid to the reserved bean mixture. Add cream and stir.

Makes One Gallon

Coal Creek Chicken with Raspberry Coulis

2 c. Spinach, blanched
1 T. Butter, unsalted
1/3 c. White wine
1/2 c. Heavy cream
1 Chicken breast, 4-oz., skinless
2 oz. Chorizo (Mexican sausage), cooked, puréed
2 T. Piñon nuts, toasted

Blanch spinach in a steamer for 2 minutes, drain and finely chop. Then sauté spinach in butter for 1 minute. Add wine and reduce completely; add cream and reduce by half. Cool.

Pound chicken breast out into a flat sheet and cover with spinach mixture. Sprinkle with chorizo and piñon nuts, roll up, and wrap with plastic wrap.

Steam in the plastic wrap for 20 minutes, remove from heat, and remove plastic wrap. Slice into 1/2-inch slices and serve atop Raspberry Coulis.

Makes One Serving

RASPBERRY COULIS:
1 qt. Raspberries, whole, frozen, thawed
1 T. Cumin
1 T. Garlic powder
2 c. Sugar
1 T. Chicken base

Combine all ingredients and simmer for 30 minutes, stirring occasionally.

Makes Six Cups

Pinon Nuts

The piñon pine is a Rocky Mountain native growing from the middle of Colorado southward. These pines are slow growing and are not very tall, commonly 15 to 25 feet. The sweet smell of piñon smoke from home heating fires perfumes the air in southern Colorado and New Mexico. It is a smell not easily forgotten. The nuts come from the cones and are gathered by spreading a blanket on the ground and shaking the tree. The Navajos are one of the primary gatherers. Piñon nuts have been consumed at least from the times of the Anasazi. They are first roasted and after the hard outer coating is removed, can be eaten whole or ground into a meal. Piñon nuts have a rich, but subtle nutty flavor that makes them a featured flavor in today's palette of Rocky Mountain cuisine.

Salmon Tamale

Sauté shrimp in olive oil for 1 minute, add piñon nuts and mint. Sauté for 1 minute longer, set aside off heat. Lay 2 corn husks down and oil the husk, then place salmon on center. Cover the salmon with the shrimp mixture, and top with garlic mayo. Place 2 corn husks on top and fold ends up. Wrap with butcher's twine. Charbroil for 10 to 15 minutes and serve.

Makes One Serving

1	Salmon, 7-oz. fillet
3 oz.	Rock shrimp (41-50 ct.), raw
1 t.	Olive oil
1/2 oz.	Piñon nuts
1/4 oz.	Brook mint
4	Corn husks
1 t.	Garlic mayo

Turtle Brownies

3/4 lb. Butter
3/4 lb. Margarine
3/4 lb. Semi-sweet chocolate
   12   Eggs, large
6-3/4 c. Sugar
   3 c. Flour
   3 c. Mixed nuts
   2 t. Vanilla
   1 lb. Cream cheese
 1/4 c. Bakers cocoa

Melt margarine and butter slowly in double boiler. Chop chocolate into small pieces and add to the butter mixture, stirring until melted. Remove from heat.

Mix 9 eggs and 5 c. of sugar until smooth. Add chocolate mixture, add flour and mix thoroughly. Add nuts and 1-1/3 t. of vanilla. Spray and dust pan with flour. Pour in brownie mixture.

Mix cream cheese until smooth. Add cocoa and remaining 1-3/4 c. of sugar. Add remaining 3 eggs, one at a time. Add remaining vanilla (2/3 t.). Swirl cream cheese mixture into brownie mixture. Bake at 300 degrees for 1-1/2 hours in preheated oven.

Makes 40 Brownies

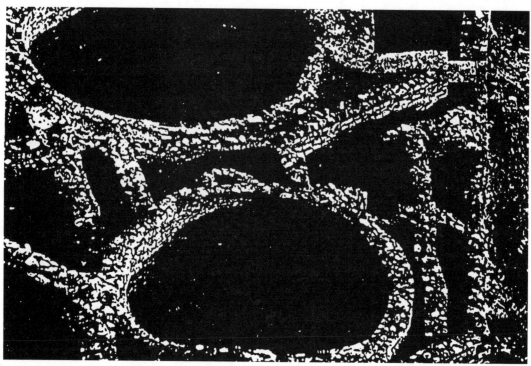

Anasazi ruins at Chaco Cultural National Historic Park southwest of Nageezi, New Mexico

Bread Pudding

Mix eggs, vanilla, and sugar together in medium-sized bowl, until sugar is dissolved (DO NOT WHIP). Add Half & Half and heavy cream until both are well blended.

In small bowl, mix sugar, cinnamon powder, and raisins.

Lay white bread in a deep dish pan and sprinkle cinnamon/sugar/raisin mixture on top. Pour liquid mixture on top of bread, push bread down when it begins to float. Soak bread thoroughly, cover pan with foil. Place on a sheet pan filled with water and bake in a pre-heated oven at 320 degrees for 1 hour or until pudding is firm on top and no liquid is showing.

May be refrigerated for about two days and reheated, cover with plastic wrap when storing in the refrigerator. Do NOT refrigerate once reheated. Serve with brandy, fruit toppings, or chocolate sauce.

14	Eggs
1/2 t.	Vanilla
2-3/4 c.	Sugar
1-1/2 qt.	Half & Half
1/2 qt.	Heavy Cream
1/2 c.	Granulated sugar
2 T.	Cinnamon powder
1 c.	Raisins, packed
6-8	Slices, white bread, toasted

Makes Eight Servings

Grub Box Thief
by Christine Burch

We were six days out of Laramie with many more to go
Drivin' 1600 head down to New Mexico.
At first I though I had misplaced those tasty little sweets,
But soon I realized I was dealing with a beast.

No, not the kind that's cute and small
Like mouse or dog or fox.
But the most dangerous kind of all —
The midnight thief of the grub box!

I had come well prepared and brought my little trap.
I tested it to check the spring, and boy how it could snap!
So I placed it down, discrete and fast, among the other treats.
I said goodnight and went to bed and feigned I was asleep.

After all had gone to bed, I heard a noise and rose
To find the thief in the grub box, a-standin' on his toes!
It wasn't long before we all heard the awful snap.
The howling critter who stole the sweets wore boots and a Stetson hat!

Brooks Lake Lodge, a log structure, was hand crafted in 1922 to accommodate travelers on their journey from the railhead in Lander, Wyoming, to Yellowstone National Park. The Brooks Lake Lodge is within the Shoshone National Forest surrounded by the Pinnacle formation of the Absoroka Mountains, the Wind River Mountains, and the Continental Divide. With two distinct seasons, winter and summer, outdoor enthusiasts seeking luxury accommodations in an unsurpassed setting will find what they are searching for at Brooks Lake. Summer visitors enjoy horseback riding, hiking, fishing, and canoeing, while winter activities focus on cross-country skiing and snowmobiling. Wildlife and wild flowers abound in the summer, and superb powder snow attracts winter visitors. Day trips to Jackson Hole, Yellowstone National Park, and Grand Teton National Park are easily arranged. The Lodge is located approximately 55 miles from Jackson Hole airport, and is served by many major airlines and rental car companies. Hotel rates include the fine cuisine.

458 Brooks Lake Rd./P.O. Box 594, Dubois, WY / Phone: 1-307-455-2121, Fax: 1-307-455-2121

Dubois ✶ WYOMING ✶ 6 Rooms & 6 Cabins

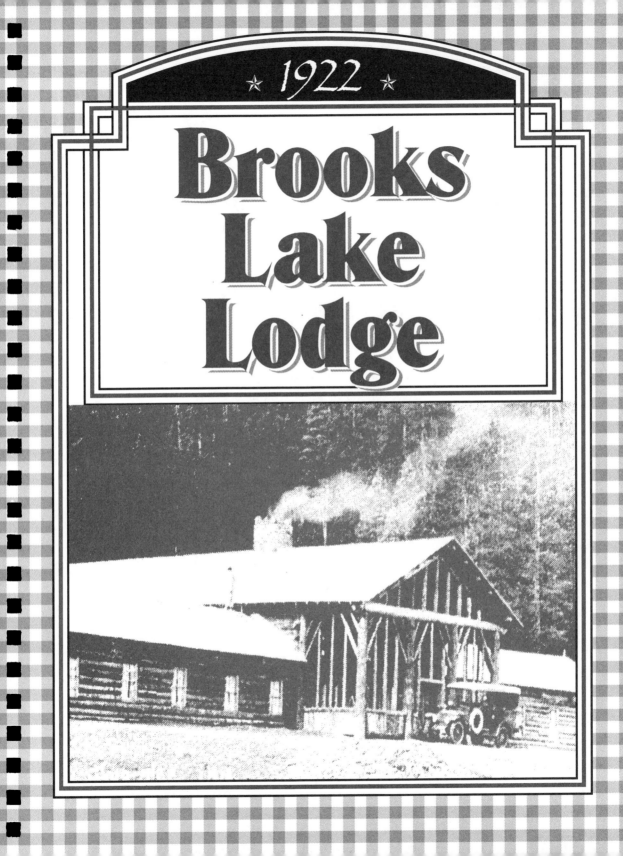

★ 1922 ★

Brooks Lake Lodge

White Onion Bisque

1/4 c.   Butter
6   White onions, large, thinly sliced
2 T.   Flour
5 c.   Chicken stock
1 c.   Whipping cream
1/8 t.   White pepper
Nutmeg, ground

In a 5-quart pan, melt butter over medium heat. Add onions and cook, stirring often, until very soft. Stir flour into onions, cook until bubbly. Add stock, whipping cream, and pepper. Bring to a boil over medium-high heat, stirring often.

Sprinkle with nutmeg before serving.

Makes Six Servings

Rack of Lamb

2   Wyoming Lamb racks, french cut
Pinch   Kosher salt
4   Garlic cloves, crushed
Thyme leaves, fresh, whole
Rosemary, fresh, chopped

Wash racks in cold water. Rub with kosher salt, garlic, thyme, and rosemary. Cook in a hot oven at 425 degrees for 20 minutes. Serve medium-rare.

Makes Two Servings

Cowboy Brunch
by Christine Burch

Cookin' for the cowboys out on a cattle drive
Ought to make a gal re-think the path she chose in life.
They grumble 'bout the biscuits, the taters and the meat,
So I figgered the next mornin' I'd cook them up a treat.

I got up extra early to softly poach the eggs,
Sauté the ham just perfect and prepare the hollandaise.
Well they et it up right quickly, then each one grabbed his hoss,
And they thanked me for the Egg McMuffins with the fancy yellow sauce!

Torta Di Zucchini

Wash the zucchini well and soak in a bowl of cold water for 30 minutes. Remove the ends from the zucchini. Thinly slice 1 pound of zucchini and coarsely grate the other pound into a small bowl with a hand grater, using the side of the grater with the large holes. Then finely grate the lemon rind. Mix the eggs and Parmesan together in a second bowl. Add the grated lemon rind, 1/4 c. of the bread crumbs, salt, and pepper to taste. Preheat the oven to 375 degrees.

Add the sliced and grated zucchini to the egg mixture, mixing very well with a wooden spoon.

Butter a 10-inch pie plate and coat it with some of the bread crumbs. Pour the zucchini mixture into the plate. Sprinkle the remaining bread crumbs over the top. Bake at 375 degrees for 35 minutes. Remove from oven and cool for a few minutes. Then put a serving plate upside down, over the torte. Turn the torte and plate right side up and remove the pie plate. Put another serving plate over the torte and turn it over so that it is now top side up.

Sprinkle with freshly ground black pepper and serve, slicing like a cake.

Makes Six to Eight Servings

2 lb.	Zucchini, small
1	Lemon rind
4	Eggs, extra large
1/4 c.	Parmesan cheese, freshly grated
1/2 c.	Bread crumbs, unseasoned, preferably homemade
	Salt, black pepper (to taste)

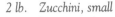

6	Roma tomatoes, halved lengthwise
6 T.	Olive oil
	Salt and pepper (to taste)
6 t.	Parsley, fresh, chopped
6	Garlic cloves, crushed
4	Tomato halves
1/2 c.	Parmesan cheese, grated
2 T.	Olive oil
2 T.	Butter
2 T.	Basil, freshed, chopped

Brush tomato halves with oil, sprinkle with salt and pepper, top equally with parsley and garlic. Bake 70 minutes in 425-degree oven. Tomatoes will get dark.

Boil your favorite pasta to al dente.

Mash together in a large bowl with a fork the tomato halves, cheese, oil, butter, and basil.

Add cooked pasta. Toss to coat. Divide on individual plates, placing 2 tomato halves on each serving.

Makes Four Servings

Sage
by Christine Burch

These hills are full of beauty, but what I like the best
> *Are the pungent strong aromas of the Rocky Mountain West.*
No, I don't mean all the critters or the smells that come with age.
> *I'm talkin' 'bout that hardy plant, the tough and noble sage.*

Some folks would like to see it gone, they think it's such a pain.
> *But have you ever smelled the sage after a summer rain?*
Have you seen it glisten with the mornin' dew
> *Or filled your lungs with its fragrance when springtime is brand new?*

I could go on forever talkin' on the sage
> *But the publisher has told me to keep it to one page.*

Chocolate Mousse Brooks Lake

Melt together the chocolate, coffee, and liqueur over steaming water, stirring occasionally.

12 oz.	Semi-sweet chocolate
1/2 c.	Strong coffee
1 oz.	Raspberry, Amaretto, or Grand Marnier liqueur

Beat egg whites and cream of tartar, until stiff peaks form. Add heavy cream, continue to beat, until it loses its gloss. Heat 3 egg yolks and slowly add to melted chocolate mixture. Slowly fold into whipped mixture. Pipe into glasses. Chill for two hours.

6	Egg whites
1/4 t.	Cream of tartar
3 c.	Heavy cream

Makes Four Servings

Paradise Cake

Mix all ingredients only until moist, pour into a bundt pan. Bake for 30 minutes at 375 degrees. Cool and frost with cream cheese frosting.

Makes Ten to Twelve Servings

2 c.	Flour
2 c.	Sugar
2	Eggs
2 t.	Baking soda
1 t.	Salt
1 t.	Vanilla
1	Pineapple, 20-oz can, crushed, undrained
1 c.	Coconut
1 c.	Nuts

Cream butter and cream cheese. Mix in powdered sugar, and beat until smooth. Add vanilla, and beat until completed mixed.

CREAM CHEESE FROSTING:

1 box	Powdered sugar
1/4 lb.	Butter, softened
8 oz.	Cream cheese
1 t.	Vanilla

The Black Hills of South Dakota are rich with the history and culture of the Old West. Part of that history is the Historic Franklin Hotel in the colorful town of Deadwood. The Franklin was built in Greek Revival-style for the then-astounding cost of $100,000. Considered so architecturally beautiful, it attracted such guests as John Wayne, Pearl Buck, Babe Ruth, and President Theodore Roosevelt. After 88 years in business, it began a meticulous $1.7 million renovation. Tin ceilings, fireplaces, pillars, and ceramic floors are all being restored to their original condition. Each room is beautifully furnished with antiques and lace curtains. Corner rooms have curved glass windows, and there is Victorian art throughout. Other guest amenities include three lounges, a veranda, a family dining room, an Irish Pub, a gift shop, and an art gallery. The Franklin is at the center of Deadwood's legalized gambling district. The nearby attractions include Mt. Rushmore, Crazy Horse Monument, Custer State Park, and there is plenty of fishing, tennis, golf, and skiing.

700 Main Street, Deadwood, SD / Phone: 1-605-578-2241, 1-800-688-1876, Fax: 1-605-578-3452

Deadwood ☆ SOUTH DAKOTA ☆ 75 Rooms

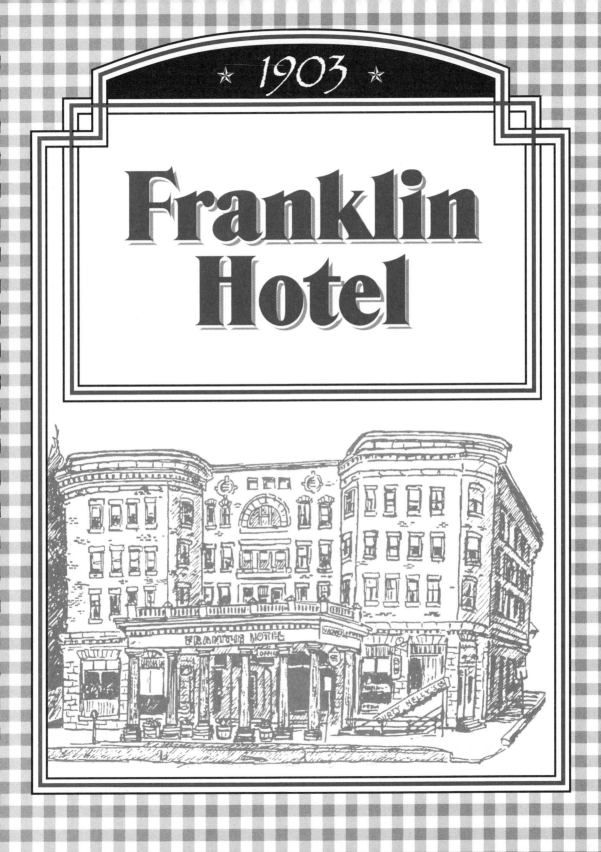

Sauteed Mushrooms

2 T.   Olive oil
1/2 T.   Garlic
1 T.   Green peppers, diced
1 T.   Red peppers, diced
1 T.   Onions, diced
8 oz.   Mushrooms, fresh
1 T.   Parmesan cheese, grated

Put all ingredients except for cheese in an 8- or 10-inch sauté pan, add mushrooms last. Sauté over high heat for about 5 minutes. Toss several times while cooking to mix ingredients.

Before serving, sprinkle with Parmesan cheese.

Makes Two Servings

Buffalo London Broil

Buffalo flank steak marinated in a special sauce. Broil to your personal specifications.

1   Buffalo flank steak, 16-oz.
    Salt, pepper (to taste)

MARINADE:
3 oz.   Tabasco sauce
2/3 c.   Oil
1/2 c.   Wine vinegar
1   Garlic clove, split
1 t.   Mustard, dry
1/2 t.   Salt
1/2 t.   Basil, dried, leaves crushed
1/2 t.   Oregano, dried, leaves
    crushed
1/4 t.   Red pepper, crushed

With a sharp knife, remove any fat and gristle from Buffalo steak. Score both sides of the steak to help tenderize. Cut Buffalo flank into two 8-oz. steaks.

Mix the marinade ingredients and chill to blend flavors. Remove the garlic and shake again. Add Buffalo steaks, cover, marinate in refrigerator overnight.

Preheat broiler and season steaks with salt and pepper to taste. Broil for 5 minutes, turn steaks and broil for 5 minutes more for rare or 6 minutes for medium. To check doneness, with a knife, make a small cut in the center of the meat. With knife in slanting position, carve 1/4-inch slices across width of steaks. Serve.

Makes Two Servings

Pineapple-Glazed Carrots

Steam baby carrots until tender. In a separate saucepan, add all remaining ingredients, and cook over medium heat, until mixture is heated to simmering. Add steamed carrots, serve.

Makes Six to Eight Servings

2 lb.	Baby carrots
1 T.	Nutmeg, cinnamon (each)
1 T.	Maple syrup, sugar, brown sugar (each)
1 T.	Vanilla
1/2 c.	Margarine
1/2 c.	Pineapple juice
5	Pineapple rings, chopped

Vegetable Bread Dinner Rolls

In a large bowl, combine sugar, salt, yeast, and 1-1/2 c. flour. In 1-quart saucepan, heat milk and butter until very warm (120-130 degrees F). With mixer at low speed, gradually beat liquid into dry ingredients. At medium speed, beat 2 minutes, occasionally scraping bowl with a rubber spatula.

Mix vegetables and seasonings for the Vegetable Mix.

Beat in eggs and about 1/2 cup flour to make a thick batter; add vegetable mix, continue beating 2 more minutes. Stir in flour (1 to 2-1/2 c.) to make a soft dough. On lightly floured surface, knead dough until smooth and elastic, about 10 minutes. Shape dough into ball. Turn in large, greased bowl to grease top. Cover and let rise in warm place until doubled, about 1 hour.

Punch down dough. Transfer to lightly floured surface, cut in half; cover and let rise 15 minutes more. Cut each half into 12 pieces; shape into balls, and place 2 inches apart on greased cookie sheets. Cover and let rise until doubled, about 30 minutes.

Preheat oven to 400 degrees. Brush with melted butter. Bake 10 minutes or until golden. Cool slightly on wire racks. Serve warm.

Makes 24 Rolls

1/3 c.	Sugar
1-1/2 t.	Salt
2 pkg.	Active dry yeast
4-1/2 to 5-1/2 c.	All purpose flour
1 c.	Milk
1/4 c.	Butter
2	Eggs

VEGETABLE MIX:

1/3 c.	Onions, finely diced
1/3 c.	Carrots, finely diced
1/3 c.	Broccoli, finely diced
1/3 c.	Celery, finely diced
2 t.	Onion powder
1 t.	Garlic, minced
	Melted butter

Mandarin Salad

1/2 c.   Almonds, sliced
3 T.   Sugar

DRESSING:
1/2 t.   Salt
Dash   Pepper
1 T.   Parsley, chopped
2 T.   Sugar
2 T.   Vinegar
Dash   Tabasco sauce

SALAD:
1/2   Iceberg lettuce, head
1/2   Romaine lettuce, head
1 c.   Celery, chopped
2   Green onions, whole, chopped

1   Mandarin oranges, 11-oz. can, drained

In a small pan over medium heat, cook almonds and sugar, stirring constantly until almonds are coated and sugar is dissolved. Watch carefully as they burn easily. Cool and set aside.

Mix salt, pepper, parsley, sugar, vinegar, and Tabasco sauce.

Mix salad ingredients just before serving, add almonds and oranges last.

Toss with dressing to taste.

Makes Four to Six Servings

The Gold Camp Hotel Menu

These western towns were founded for various reasons — railhead for shipping, supply point for miners, the only place with water to grow crops, or gold. Deadwood is one of several of these so called gold camps up and down the Rockies. Others are in this book — Leadville, Cripple Creek, and Empire, for example. All shared common characteristics. Gold fever drew people from all over the country, indeed, from around the world. They lusted for the gold to provide them a way out. Many lost. Many prospered.

The miners wanted their culture and fine theater, melodramas, and opera abounded. Deadwood had multiple theatres and nearby Lead, an Opera House. The best place to dine in these gold camps was always the big hotel. Many of the miners had gold in their pockets and wanted to have a big night out — to feel special. So naturally, the finest hotel served up cuisine rather than vittles. Special events, like the Fourth of July, had menus which would do any big coast city place proud today.

Hey, Cookie!

by Christine Burch

"Hey, Cookie!" they would call to me
　　Several times a day.
"What's fer supper? Somethin' good?"
　　Was all they had to say.

I really didn't mind the talk
　　It wasn't all that bad.
'Cuz anything I cooked for them
　　Was the best they ever had.

You see, I was the only woman
　　For nearly fifty mile
And they's do anything for me
　　For just a meal and a smile!

The selection of appetizers usually ran to twenty or thirty. Oysters were very big, so were small birds, such as quail and pigeon. Soups often mirrored main courses so nothing would be wasted. If pheasant was an entrée, some variety of pheasant-based soup would also be on the menu. French cuisine was all the rage, so french onion soup was frequently featured. The Hotel De Paris in Georgetown, Colorado, next door to Empire, was affectionately known as Frenchy's and would draw folks from the entire territory. Salads were a bit sparse, but were more than made up for with entrées. Birds on the menu often included pheasant, duck, goose, turkey, chicken. Game meats, such as venison, antelope, elk, and buffalo, were required. Every beef dish, including occasional organ dish, were expected in cattle country. Fish included trout, bass, catfish, and pike, and this did not mean for the diner to decide if he or she felt like eating beef or game bird or fish — it meant to select one of each! Desserts were heavy on berry dishes, fruit pies, and poached fruits. French wine was a required accompaniment. An after-dinner cigar was enjoyed by the men, and an occasional woman (Poker Alice of Deadwood was famous for always having a cigar in her mouth).

After a meal such as this, it's no wonder that the patent medicine salesman had a lively business in nostrum, elixirs, and digestives!

Fully restored to its original 1920s splendor, the Gallatin Gateway Inn is among the finest inns in the Rocky Mountain West. Designed to be a grand railroad hotel, this palatial structure features arched windows, Spanish-style corbels, and carved beams. The original railroad clock still keeps accurate time in the lobby. Rooms and suites are decorated in the warm, clean tones of the West and offer the conveniences required by today's busy traveler. The Inn's spacious restaurant, a local favorite, is well known for its Rocky Mountain cuisine. There are conference and banquet facilities on site. The Inn's unusual amenities include a fly casting pond in its own back yard, mountain bikes, tennis courts, swimming pool, and hot tub are all enjoyed by guests. Gallatin Gateway's staff is renowned for its western hospitality. The Inn is located minutes from excellent fishing, horseback riding, hunting, hiking, and downhill and cross-country skiing. Also nearby are Yellowstone National Park and Grand Teton National Park.

P.O. Box 376, Gallatin Gateway, MT / Phone: 1-406-763-4672, 1-800-676-3522; Fax: 1-406-763-4672 x. 313

Gallatin Gateway ★ MONTANA ★ 25 Rooms

✫ 1927 ✫

Gallatin Gateway Inn

Chicken Liver Pate

2-1/4 lbs.	Chicken livers
3	Eggs
2-1/4 oz.	Shallots
3 oz.	Brandy
2 t.	Salt
1/2 t.	Pepper
2 lb.+2 oz.	Butter, softened
1/2 c.	Flour, sifted
1-1/4 c.	Heavy cream
1/2 lb.	Lard, melted (optional)

In a food processor, purée the chicken livers, eggs, shallots, brandy, salt, and pepper for 5 minutes. While processing, combine the softened butter and flour. Add to liver mixture. Add heavy cream last. Line mold with plastic wrap.

Place liver mixture in mold, cover with foil. Place mold in roasting pan with water one-third of the way up the side of the mold. Bake in 250-degree oven to an internal temperature of 140 degrees. Remove from waterbath. Let cool and cover with melted lard, if you wish. Refrigerate overnight.

To Serve: Unmold and slice.

Makes One Pâté

Simple Bruschetta

2 - 3	Slices of sourdough bread
	Garlic infused olive oil (or
	virgin olive oil)
	French goat cheese

Tomato/Basil Mixture:

3	Roma tomatoes, chopped
1/2 T.	Garlic, fresh, chopped
1/2 t.	Black pepper, coarse ground
1/2 t.	Kosher salt
1-1/2 T.	Olive oil
1-1/2 T.	Basil, fresh, chopped

Brush medium slices of sourdough bread with garlic infused olive oil (or virgin olive oil) and toast. Spread with a thin layer of aged French goat cheese.

Mix roma tomatoes, garlic, pepper, salt, olive oil, and basil.

To Serve: Top with a generous amount of tomato/basil mixture and garnish with a sprig of fresh basil.

Makes Four Servings

Buffalo Ribeye

Mix water, beer, honey, chile powder, pepper, and garlic.

Marinate steaks for 24 hours. Grill steaks slowly over medium heat.

Makes Four Servings

4   Buffalo ribeye steaks, 8-10 oz. each, fresh

MARINADE:
- 8 oz.   Water
- 8 oz.   Light beer
- 1 T.   Honey
- 2 T.   Ancho chile powder
- 1 t.   Black pepper, coarsely ground
- 3   Garlic cloves, fresh, diced

Montana-Stuffed Trout Pecan

COATING: Mixture of ground pecans and white flour, seasoned with salt and pepper.

In another bowl, mix the stuffing ingredients: onion, pepper, corn, oregano, thyme, and cornbread crumbs.

Dip trout in cold milk and lightly coat with pecan/flour mixture, stuff, and pan sauté slowly in clarified butter.

Makes One Serving

1   Montana Trout, fresh medium-sized with head on
    Milk, cold
    Butter, clarified

COATING:
- Pecans, ground
- White flour
- Salt, pepper (to taste)

STUFFING:
- 1   Onion, whole white, diced
- 1   Red bell pepper, large, diced
- 1 c.   Whole corn
- 1 T.   Oregano, fresh
- 1 T.   Thyme, fresh
- 3 c.   Cornbread, dry crumbled

Pork Chops with Cambazola Crust

4 Pork chops, double thick
1 oz. Olive oil

MARINADE:
1/3 Onion, yellow, diced
1/2 t. Chili flakes
1/2 oz. Red wine
1/2 oz. Lemon juice
2 oz. Virgin olive oil
1/4 t. Black pepper, fresh ground
1/2 t. Thyme, chopped

CAMBAZOLA CRUST:
1/2 lb. Cambazola cheese
1 oz. Piñon nuts
1 t. Thyme, chopped
Salt and pepper (to taste)

Place onion, chili flakes, red wine, lemon juice, olive oil in a bowl and mix until smooth. Coat pork chops with the marinade mixture. Cover. Marinate overnight.

In a food processor, purée cambazola cheese, piñon nuts, thyme, salt, and pepper to a smooth paste. Set aside.

Remove chops from marinade and pat dry. Heat a large sauté pan with 1 oz. of oil, until it just starts to smoke. Place chops in pan and fry until golden brown, both sides. Then place into 400-degree oven for 10 minutes. Remove pork from oven when juice just starts to turn clear when pricked with skewer. The meat should feel firm and spring back when touched. Turn oven to Broil.

Spread cambazola cheese mixture onto pork and return to oven. Glaze under broiler until golden.

Makes Four Servings

Garlic Mashed Potatoes

3 oz. Olive oil
4 Garlic cloves, whole
1/2 c. Heavy cream or milk
3 T. Butter
2 lbs. Idaho potatoes, peeled, boiled, strained, mashed
Salt and pepper (to taste)

In a small saucepan, add oil and garlic; bring to a slow simmer, until garlic is very soft and can be crushed with a fork. Strain. Crush garlic into a paste with a fork.

In a medium, thick-bottom pot, add cream and butter. Bring to a simmer. Add potatoes and incorporate cream and butter with a wooden spoon. Add garlic paste. Heat mixture, stir while heating. Season with salt and pepper.

Place garlic potatoes onto center of plate. Place cambazola-crusted pork chops leaning up against potatoes and serve.

Makes Four Servings

Strawberry and Blueberry Cobbler

Preheat oven to 350 degrees. Toss fruit in 1 T. sugar. Line the bottom of a dessert baking dish with the fruit. Sift flour and baking powder together. Combine sugar, eggs, milk, vanilla extract, and lemon rind to make a batter. Pour batter over fruit. Bake in 350-degree oven for 30 minutes or until golden brown.

Makes Eight Servings

1 c.	Strawberries, fresh
1 c.	Blueberries, fresh
1 T.	Sugar (to toss fruit)
2 c.	Flour
1-1/4 t.	Baking powder
2 c.	Sugar
4	Eggs, beaten
1-1/2 c.	Milk
2 t.	Vanilla extract
2 t.	Lemon rind, grated

Strawberry Devonshire

A wonderfully simple dessert, in which you can substitute your favorite summer berry for the strawberries.

Toss together strawberries, sugar, sherry, and orange zest.

2 pt.	Strawberries, sliced
1/4 c.	Sugar
1	Shot of sherry
1	Orange, zested, chopped fine

DEVONSHIRE CREAM:

6 oz.	Mascarpone (Italian cream cheese)
1-3/4 c.	Heavy whipping cream
1/2 t.	Vanilla extract
2 T.	Sugar

In another bowl, whip the Mascarpone, whipping cream, vanilla extract, and sugar, until it forms soft peaks.

TO SERVE: Spoon berries into a decorative glass and top with the Devonshire cream.

Makes Four Servings

Ginger Mascarpone Cheesecake

From Jill Hamilton, pastry chef, who has worked and developed her pastry skills in Washington, DC; Cleveland, OH; Lucerne, Switzerland; and Bordeaux, France; and returned to her hometown of Bozeman in 1989 to join our talented team of chefs.

CRUST:

1-1/2 c.	Chocolate cookie crumbs
1/4 c.	Sugar
3 oz.	Butter, melted

Mix crumbs with sugar and add melted butter. Press into bottom of 9-inch springform pan.

CHEESECAKE:

1-1/2 c.	Sugar
2 T.	Cream cheese
1/2 lb.	Mascarpone (Italian cream cheese)
2	Eggs
1-1/2 T.	Ginger root, fresh, ground

Cream sugar, cream cheese, and Mascarpone. Add eggs and ginger. Spread batter into pan and bake in 300-degree oven for 20 to 25 minutes. Refrigerate until cold.

Makes One Cake

Carmen's Marnier Pudding

1/2 c.	Amaretto cookies
2 T.	Espresso or strong coffee
1-1/4 lbs.	Cream cheese
2/3 c.	Sugar
2	Eggs
1 T.	Grand Marnier
1 t.	Rum

Crumble the amaretto cookies, pour in the coffee, and let stand until saturated.

Combine cream cheese, sugar, eggs, Grand Marnier, rum, and cookie mixture. Whip on medium to high speed until all lumps are gone.

Spoon into serving dishes and chill for at least 2 hours.

Makes Six Servings

Chocolate Ganache Tart with Caramel Sauce

Cut in butter into flour and cinnamon in food processor. Add nuts and process until a 'dough' forms. Press into a tart pan and bake in 350-degree oven for 15 minutes.

Scald cream, then stir chocolate in to melt. Whisk in the eggs yolks, cooking for 1 minute. Stir in coffee, vanilla, and butter. Pour into the crust and let set.

Melt together the brown sugar, butter, and corn syrup and simmer for 8 to 10 minutes. Cool for 15 minutes and add cream. Keep warm and serve on plate with tart slice.

Makes Eight Servings

CRUST:
1/3 c.	Butter
1-1/2 c.	Flour
1 t.	Cinnamon
1/2 c.	Pecans

FILLING:
2 c.	Cream
16 oz.	Chocolate
4	Egg yolks
1 T.	Coffee
1 t.	Vanilla
4 oz.	Butter

CARAMEL SAUCE:
4 c.	Brown sugar
2 c.	Butter
2-2/3 c.	Corn syrup
1-1/3 c.	Cream

Sour Cherry-Almond Bread Pudding

Preheat over to 350 degrees. Line a buttered, medium-size baking dish with stale bread. Combine all the remaining ingredients and whisk until incorporated. Cover the bread with the liquid mixture, evenly distributing cherries and nuts. Cover with foil.

Place baking dish in a pan of hot water in the 350-degree oven for about 45 minutes or until firm. Cool slightly, serve warm.

Makes Six Servings

3 - 4 c.	Stale bread
1 oz.	Maderia
3 c.	Milk
3	Egg yolks, beaten
1/2 c.	Sugar
1 t.	Vanilla
1/2 t.	Nutmeg
1/2 c.	Sour cherries, dried
1/4 c.	Almonds, chopped

The Irma is a living museum of the Old West. Town father, Buffalo Bill Cody, built and named the hotel for his daughter, Irma. There are fifteen original suites featuring Victorian-period furnishings and twenty-five other guestrooms. Of particular note is The Irma's ornate cherrywood back bar, a gift from Queen Victoria to Buffalo Bill, which is a focus of the main dining room. Cody used profits from his Wild West Shows to haul his treasure west. The Irma offers three meeting room sizes, including rooms for intimate seminars; the Governor's Room for banquets of up to 60 people, and the Main Dining Room for banquets of up to 200. When you step into The Irma, you step into the friendliness and hospitality of the 19th-century West. The Irma is within walking distance to the famous Buffalo Bill Historical Center, shopping, river floats, and golf course, and is just minutes from fishing, big game hunting, pack trips, and wind surfing. Within one-hour's drive is Yellowstone National Park. During the summer season, there is a nightly rodeo and a special 4th of July celebration, that adds to the Wild West character of Cody.

1192 Sheridan Ave., Cody, WY / Phone: 1-307-587-4221, 1-800-745-4762, Fax: 1-307-587-4221 x. 21

Cody ✳ WYOMING ✳ 40 Rooms

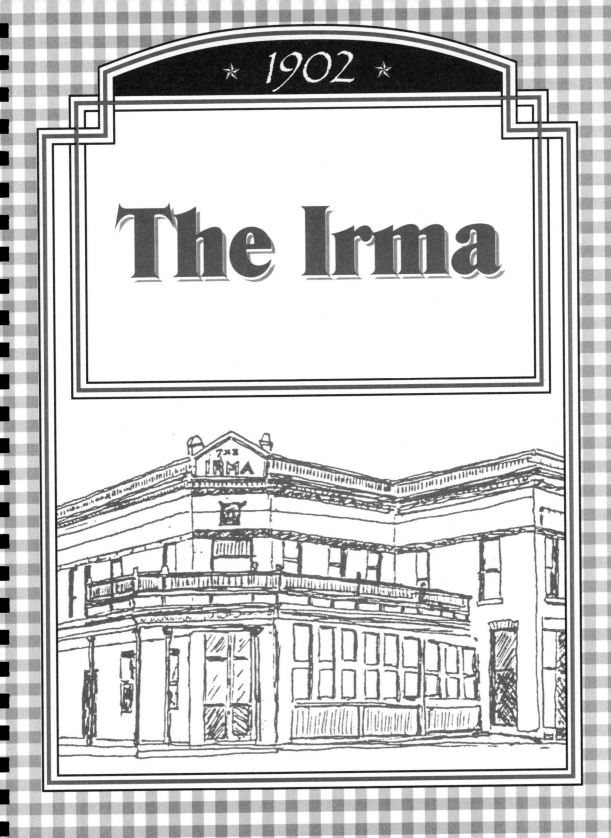

★ 1902 ★

The Irma

1/2 lb.	Bacon, chopped
1	Onion, small, chopped
2 c.	Spinach, chopped
2 cans	Oysters or 1c. of fresh oysters
1/2 t.	Salt
1 c.	Heavy cream
2 c.	Crackers, crushed
2 T.	Lemon juice
1 c.	Swiss cheese, grated

Place chopped bacon in sauté pan. Fry until half cooked, add onion and chopped spinach. Cut oysters in half and add to the sauté pan. Add salt and cook about 5 minutes. Add cream and cook another 2 minutes.

In baking dish, layer bottom with 1 c. crushed crackers. Pour mixture in, then sprinkle remaining crackers over the top. Sprinkle swiss cheese over all. Bake in 350-degree oven for about 20 minutes.

Makes Four Servings

Oysters

Oysters, fresh oysters, in the Rockies, and in the mid-1800s? Yes. Naturally, you wonder how it was done.

First, the oysters were packed in wooden barrels, then, early reports indicate these barrels were placed in larger barrels with the "gap" between the barrels packed with sawdust as insulation. The oysters were packed into the inner barrel, with their hinged ends down, so that they could more easily take in through the opening the cornmeal with which they were fed. The freight wagons would stop regularly to renew the ice from local ice houses. As the ice melted, the oysters ate the cornmeal.

Fresh oysters have always been considered a special aspect of the Rocky Mountain cuisine. As is true for many aspects of this cuisine, immigrants brought their own food cultures along, and Easterners brought oysters. Early photographs of Deadwood, South Dakota, show a whole restaurant/saloon dedicated to the oyster called the "Oyster Bay." Today, you can still find the "Oyster Bay" in Deadwood, reincarnated by a transplanted New Jersey shoreman serving fresh oysters that are now brought by jet; a bit quicker than the prairie freighters of the mid-1800s.

Today, it still surprises the visitor to the Rockies that the region can have fresh seafood. The regional fresh food wholesalers serving these hotels buy on the coasts very early in the day and jet their catch to the region by mid-morning. We can literally have the morning's market fish on our table that evening.

Fish in a Bag

Place fish in center of parchment paper and arrange mushrooms, cherry tomato halves, lemon and green pepper slices on and around filet. Fold edges of paper up to prevent contents from escaping. Pour Mountain Dew over filet and finish folding paper so you create an enclosed bag around the fish. Staple paper closed, if need be.

Bake in 375-degree oven for 16 to 18 minutes. Serve in the bag.

Makes One Serving

1	White meat fish filet, 7 to 8 oz.
1	Parchment paper (~ 20 x 14 inches), freezer wrap will work
4	Mushrooms, medium, whole
2	Cherry tomatoes, halved
	Lemon slices
	Green pepper slices
2 oz.	Mountain Dew

Outback Curried Lamb Stew

Dice lamb into 1-inch chunks and brown in a fry pan or skillet in hot olive oil. Dice the vegetables into 1-inch chunks. Slowly add flour to lamb chunks, forming a gravy of sorts. You must stir constantly while adding the flour. Add the vegetables to mixture, then add the seasonings: cayenne pepper, garlic, salt, curry powder, paprika, nutmeg. Cook and stir for 4 to 5 minutes. Now add the water, and simmer until vegetables are tender, but firm.

Makes Eight Servings

2 lbs.	Lamb, 1-inch chunks
8 T.	Olive oil
4	Carrots, medium
2	Onions, medium
4	Celery stalks
2	Potatoes, large
2	Turnips
1/2 c.	Flour
1/8 t.	Cayenne pepper
2	Garlic cloves
1/2 t.	Salt
2 t.	Curry powder
2 t.	Paprika
1 t.	Nutmeg
2-1/4 c.	Water

Peanut Butter Pie

8 oz. Cream cheese, soft
1 c. Peanut butter
1 T. Vanilla
2/3 c. Sugar
1 Graham cracker crust

TOPPING:
1 oz. Semi-sweet chocolate
2 T. Margarine
1/2 c. Sour cream
1 t. Vanilla
Sugar (to make sweet enough)

Cream together cream cheese and peanut butter. Add vanilla and sugar. Pour into graham cracker crust and bake in 350-degree oven for 20 minutes.

Melt chocolate in margarine. Mix in sour cream, vanilla, and enough sugar to sweeten.

Pour topping over pie and chill for four hours.

Makes Six Servings

Banana Nut Cake

2 Eggs
1-1/2 c. Milk
1 c. Oil
2/3 c. Brown sugar
2-1/2 c. Flour
1 t. Salt
3 t. Baking powder
2 c. Bananas, mashed
1 c. Nuts, chopped

Mix together eggs, milk, oil, and brown sugar. Set aside. Mix well flour, salt, baking powder, mashed bananas, and nuts, and add to egg-milk mixture. Lightly grease a 13 x 9 x 2-inch pan.

Bake in 350-degree oven for 30 to 35 minutes or till a toothpick comes out clean.

Makes Eight Servings

Dissolve the yeast in warm water. Add the sugar, salt, cooled milk, eggs, cinnamon, and melted butter. Mix well.

Add the flour, 1 cup at a time, until dough is easy to handle. Place dough on a floured surface and knead until the dough is not sticky, add more flour if necessary.

Place kneaded dough in a greased bowl and let rise until doubled, punch down and let rise until doubled again. Punch down again and then roll dough on flat surface into a rectangular shape, approximately 3/8-inches thick.

Spread softened margarine over dough to completely cover it. Generously sprinkle brown sugar onto the margarine to completely cover. Tightly roll the dough up and cross cut into 12 pieces.

Place pieces on greased pan, let rise until doubled and bake in a 375-degree oven for 15 minutes or until golden brown.

Mix the glaze ingredients together and add warm water to get desired consistancy. Glaze the rolls while they are still slightly warm.

Makes Twelve Servings

2 T.	Yeast
1/2 c.	Water, warm
1/2 c.	Sugar
2 t.	Salt
1-1/2 c.	Milk, scalded, and cooled
2	Eggs
1 t.	Cinnamon
1/2 c.	Butter, melted, cooled
~ 7 c.	Flour
	Margarine
	Brown sugar

GLAZE:

8 oz.	Cream cheese, softened
2 c.	Powdered sugar
1 t.	Vanilla
1 t.	Cinnamon
1/4 c.	Buttermilk

A million acres of wilderness with jagged peaks, wildlife, and glaciers awaits travelers to the Izaak Walton Inn, adjacent to Glacier National Park. Originally built to accommodate Great Northern Railway crews, today the Inn welcomes Amtrak passengers detraining at its front door or visitors arriving by car. The lobby brings Montana's sculptured landscape indoors with a massive stone fireplace, log furniture, and pine ceilings. Rooms are appointed with American quilts, Montana-pine furniture, and antique school desks, with historic memorabilia of the Inn and Park. Guests mingle around the lobby fireplace prior to dining on brook trout, Montana beef, or Rocky Mountain specials. Families enjoy the lounge-recreation room and the Inn's European Plan skiing and hiking packages. The Izaak Walton Inn is a beautiful historic chalet where guests repair after a day's sojourn viewing mountain goat, elk, and moose. Glacier National Park is a quarter-mile by auto, foot, skis, or horseback. Walton Goat Lick provides a close look at wildlife.

P.O. Box 653, Essex, MT / Phone: 1-406-888-5700, Fax: 1-406-888-5200

Essex ☆ MONTANA ☆ 31 Rooms & 4 Caboose

1939 ★

Izaak Walton Inn

Oriental Chicken Salad

ORIENTAL SAUCE:

2 c.	Pineapple juice
1/4 c.	Soy sauce
1/4 c.	Brown sugar
1/4 c.	Water
1/4 c.	Cornstarch
1/2 c.	Oyster sauce
1/2 c.	Creamy Italian Dressing
6 oz.	Mushrooms
6 oz.	Water chestnuts
2 T.	Sesame oil
4	Chicken breasts
	Canola oil
	Garden greens
	Sprouts
	Carrots, shredded
	Cherry tomatoes

Bring to a boil the pineapple juice, soy sauce, and brown sugar. In a separate container, mix the water and cornstarch to form a roux. Slowly add roux to boiling mixture, until it reaches the consistency of a thick gravy. Remove from the heat. Then add oyster sauce and Italian Dressing. Blend with a whisk and set aside.

In a skillet, sauté the mushrooms and water chestnuts in the sesame oil. Drain any excess oil and add to the thickened sauce.

Grill the chicken breasts in canola oil. Julienne the breasts into 1/4-inch strips. Place over a dinner-size plate of garden greens, garnish with sprouts, shredded carrots, and cherry tomatoes. Top with desired amount of Oriental Sauce.

Makes Four Servings

Beef Barley Soup

1-1/4 lb.	Beef short ribs, cut in pieces
6 c.	Water
1 T.	Margarine
1 c.	Onions, chopped
1/2 c.	Celery, diced
1/2 lb.	Mushrooms, fresh, sliced
1 t.	Garlic, finely minced
1/3 c.	Burgundy wine
1/2 c.	Barley, medium
1 T.	Beef base
1 t.	Salt
Dash	Pepper
1	Bay leaf
1/4 c.	Parsley, chopped

Boil beef in the water until tender, about 2 hours. Skim and remove the meat and set aside to cool; reserve the broth. In a skillet, melt the margarine. Add the onion, celery, mushrooms, and garlic. Cook until onion is golden, about 5 to 10 minutes.

Remove the meat from the bones and add to the broth, along with the wine, barley, and seasonings and simmer, covered until the barley is cooked, about 30 minutes. Refrigerate overnight, then remove as much of the solidified fat as possible.

TO SERVE: Heat the soup.

Makes Six Servings

Izaak Walton House Dressing

Combine all ingredients, except oil in blender and mix well, stopping as necessary to scrape down sides of container. With machine running, gradually pour in oil, blending until dressing is creamy. Transfer to container with tight-fitting lid and refrigerate before using. Whisk or shake if dressing separates on standing, or reblend.

1/2 c.	Onion, finely chopped
1/4 c.	Cider vinegar
1/4 c.	Sugar
1/2 t.	Salt
1/2 t.	Mustard, dry
1/4 t.	Celery seed
1/2 c.	Oil

Makes One Cup

Huckleberry Chicken

4	Chicken breast (approx. 5 oz.), boneless, grilled

Boil water, sugar, lemon juice, nutmeg, salt, and cornstarch and water (mixed to make the roux). Cook until mixture turns semi-transparent. Stir in the berries, and cook until thickened, but not too long to overcook the berries.

HUCKLEBERRY SAUCE:

1 c.	Water
1/4 c.	Sugar
1 t.	Lemon juice
Dash	Nutmeg
	Salt (to taste)
1 T.	Cornstarch
1 T.	Water
1/4 c.	Huckleberries

Melt butter, then add the flour to form a roux. Separately heat the milk and whipping cream, until just below a boil (use care not to BOIL). Add roux and blend and cook until correct consistency. Add the wine, salt, and parmesan cheese.

FETTUCINI SAUCE:

3/4 c.	Real butter
1-1/2 c.	Flour
6 c.	Milk
1 qt.	Whipping cream
1/2 t.	Garlic, granulated
1/2 c.	White wine
2 t.	Salt
2 T.	Parmesan cheese

TO SERVE: Place a grilled chicken breast on top of the fettucini in a cream sauce. Pour 1 oz. of Huckleberry sauce over the chicken breast.

Serve with side dish of fresh vegetables — your choice.

Makes Four Servings

Western-Style Baked Salmon

2 Salmon filets, 8-oz.
6 Lemon slices
Dash Dill
Dash Lawry's Seasoning Salt

HERB BUTTER LOG:
Butter
Lemon juice
Dill
Pimento, chopped
Garlic, minced

Flour the skin side of the salmon filet. Place on a buttered sheet pan. Season meat side of filet with a dash of dill and dash of Lawry's Seasoning Salt. Place three slices of lemon (spread out) over each filet and cook in 350-degree oven for about 20 minutes, until the salmon flakes apart in the center.

Serve with a side dish of lemon-butter dipping sauce or a pat of Herb Butter Log.

This dish is nicely complimented by wild rice and steamed asparagus.

Makes Two Servings

Orange Sponge Cake

8 Eggs (1 c. whites)
1-1/3 c. Orange juice
1/2 t. Salt
1-1/2 t. Orange rind, grated
3/4 t. Cream of tartar
1 t. Lemon extract
1-1/3 c. Cake flour, sifted

Beat egg whites with cream of tartar and salt, until they hold a point. Beat egg yolks until thick and lemon colored. Gradually beat in sugar to egg yolks. Beat in part of juice, flavoring, rind, and flour, then remaining juice. Gently fold whites into egg yolk mixture. Pour into ungreased tube cake pan. Bake in 325-degree oven for 65 minutes.

Makes One Tube Cake

Huckleberry Pie

Combine all ingredients, except the pastry shell and crust, and let soak while making pie crust. Pour the berry mixture into the crust and dot with butter. Bake 15 minutes in 425-degree oven, then decrease to 350 degrees and bake 20 minutes longer.

Makes One Pie

4 c.	Huckleberries
1/2 c.	Brown sugar
1/4 c.	White sugar
1/4 t.	Salt
1 t.	Cinnamon
5 T.	Tapioca or 1/4 c. cornstarch
1	Pastry shell, 10-inch, unbaked
1	Crust for top

Huckleberry Cheesecake Pie

Combine the berries, sugar, cinnamon, lemon juice, and cornstarch. Bring to a boil and boil 1 minute until cornstarch is clear. Set aside to cool.

3-1/2 c.	Huckleberries
2/3 c.	White sugar
1/2 t.	Cinnamon
2 t.	Lemon juice
5 T.	Cornstarch
1	Unbaked 10-inch pie shell

Blend cream cheese, sugar, and salt. Then add eggs, one at a time, and mix thoroughly. Blend in milk and vanilla. Place cooled berry mixture into bottom of an unbaked pie shell. Gently spoon the cream cheese mixture over berries. Sprinkle with chopped walnuts. Bake in 400-degree oven for 10 minutes, then at 325 degrees for 50 minutes.

Makes One Pie

TOPPING:

8 oz.	Cream cheese, softened
1/2 c.	Sugar
1/2 t.	Salt
2	Eggs
1/2 c.	Milk
1/2 t.	Vanilla
1/8 c.	Walnuts, finely chopped

Never Fail Pie Crust

Use pie cutter to blend together the Crisco, flour, and salt. Mix together the beaten egg, water, and vinegar, and add to the flour mixture. Use as needed.

Makes Two Double-Crust Pies, or Three Single 10"

1-1/4 c.	Crisco
3 c.	Flour
1 t.	Salt
1	Egg, beaten
1/3 c.	Water
1 T.	Vinegar

Pumpkin Brandy Cheesecake

1-1/2 c.   Gingersnap cookie crumbs
1/3 c.   Almonds, sliced
1/3 c.   Margarine, melted
1/2 t.   Cinnamon

10-inch   Springform pan

CHEESECAKE:
32 oz.   Cream cheese, softened
1-1/4 c.   Sugar
1-1/2 t.   Pumpkin pie spice
1/2 t.   Ginger, ground
4   Eggs
1 c.   Pumpkin, mashed
1/4 c.   Brandy
3 T.   Half & Half

TOPPING:
2 c.   Sour cream
1/4 c.   Sugar
2 T.   Brandy

Mix together the cookie crumbs, almonds, margarine, and cinnamon, and press into springform 10-inch pan, and bake in 325-degree oven for 10 minutes.

With electric mixer, blend cream cheese, sugar, pie spice, ginger, eggs, pumpkin, brandy, and Half & Half. Pour over crust, and bake in 325-degree oven for 40 minutes. Turn oven off and let cool completely without opening oven door.

Combine sour cream, sugar, and brandy. Pour over completely cooled cheesecake and bake in 400-degree oven for 10 minutes. Cool and refrigerate. Remove from pan and press sliced almonds on sides.

Makes One Cake

Hot Buttered Rum

After mixing all the ingredients, freeze batter. When ready to use, mix 1 shot of dark rum with 2 tablespoons of batter. Fill rest of cup with hot water.

Makes Twelve Servings

2-1/2 c.	Brown sugar
4 c.	Powdered sugar
1 lb.	Butter
1 qt.	Vanilla ice cream
2 T.	Cinnamon
1 T.	Nutmeg

Rocky Mountain Apple Bread

In a large bowl, beat eggs, sugar, buttermilk, mayonnaise, and vanilla, until smooth. In another bowl, mix flour, salt, baking powder, baking soda, and cinnamon. Add to egg mixture, stir just until combined.

Core apples and chop. Add to batter with raisins and nuts; stir just to mix. Spread batter evenly in two greased and floured 5 x 9-inch loaf pans. Bake in 375-degree oven until a slender wooden pick inserted in center comes out clean, about 1 hour and 10 minutes. Cool in pan for 10 minutes, then turn out onto a rack to cool completely.

Serve with fresh fruit. Makes a wonderful appetizer.

Makes Two Loaves

4	Eggs, large
2 c.	Sugar
1/2 c.	Buttermilk
1/2 c.	Mayonnaise
1 t.	Vanilla
3-1/2 c.	White flour
1/4 t.	Salt
1 t.	Baking powder
1/2 t.	Baking soda
1 t.	Cinnamon, ground
2	Tart green apples, medium size
1 c.	Raisins
1 c.	Walnuts, chopped

Afterword

The Association of Historic Hotels of the Rocky Mountain West was formed in 1983 by a group of independent owners of properties on the National Register of Historic Places; hotels with character, personalities, and lives of their own. The owners' goals were to protect, preserve, and restore these local and national landmarks; to emphasize their history, diverse architecture and cultures; and to treasure the nearby resources, such as national and state parks and monuments.

The membership of AHH West has grown from 15 hotels in 1984 to its current size of 24 unique properties. Many of the newer members of AHH West were either not open or in distressed conditions when the original group formed. By developing and sharing marketing strategies which emphasize the hotels' character and individuality, by designing tours to promote the history and natural resources of the Rockies, and by sharing operational and technical expertise, the AHH West hotels have improved themselves and brought this true Western experience to many people who would never have considered a stay in "an old hotel." They have provided guidance to new owners of classic properties to revitalize a part of our important Western heritage. AHH West was among the first of the groups of historic lodging properties which are now seen throughout the country.

Today, AHH West hotels offer guests a wide variety of amenities, including conference, wedding, and banquet facilities; award-winning theatre, fine arts, and entertainment; and fine dining with menus as varied as the cultures and scenery of the Rockies. The region has a rich Hispanic tradition, as well as the cultures of the Native Americans, working cowboys, the miners, and the early railroad tycoons. Each hotel is ready to point out local museums, tribal ceremonies, archaeological and historic sites. AHH West hotels provide an exceptional experience for their guests in elegant and unique surroundings.

Join us and become a part of our history!

Index